CAUGHT READING

Assessment Manual

Sharon Cook
and
Kathie Babigian

PEARSON

About the Program Consultants:

Sharon Cook is a certified reading specialist who has taught at all levels, from elementary through college. She has developed and taught a reading lab for at-risk readers, chaired the California Association of Teachers Convention, and served on that association's board. She finished her public school education career as a language arts coordinator for a large school district in California, working primarily with teachers in grades 4–12. Although she is officially retired, Sharon writes and consults with teachers on helping students become successful readers and presents workshops on reading strategies. Sharon is the co-author of Secondary Reading Assessment Inventory for Middle and High School Students.

Kathie Babigian has taught grades K–8. In middle school, she expanded Reciprocal Teaching into a process that could be implemented across the curriculum, adding a variety of effective practices and literacy strategies. Kathie is currently the coordinator of the Literacy Training Center, which offers staff development to teachers from all parts of California in literacy strategies for struggling readers. In addition, Kathie travels throughout California training teachers. Kathie is the co-author of Secondary Reading Assessment Inventory for Middle and High School Students.

Grateful acknowledgment is made to the following for copyrighted material:

Allyn and Bacon Inc.: "The Names Test of Decoding" by Patricia M. Cunningham from *Phonics They Use: Words For Reading And Writing, 3e*. Published by Allyn and Bacon, Boston, MA. Copyright © 2000 by Pearson Education. Reprinted by permission of the publisher.

Prentice Hall: "Elementary Spelling Inventory 1" from *Words Their Way: Word Study For Phonics, Vocabulary And Spelling Instruction* by Donald Bear and Marcia Invernizzi. Copyright © 2000 by Prentice Hall. Used by permission.

Thank you to Nancy Harris for her guidance in the area of fluency.

Photo Credits: Cover images (left to right, top to bottom) © Photodisc/Getty Images, © Photodisc/Getty Images, © Photodisc/Getty Images, © PhotoAlto, © Ingram Publishing, © Photodisc/Getty Images, © Photodisc/Getty Images, © Ingram Publishing.

Note: Every effort has been made to locate the copyright owner of material reproduced in this component. Omissions brought to our attention will be corrected in subsequent editions.

Staff Credits: Joshua Adams, Melania Benzinger, Karen Blonigen, Laura Chadwick, Andreea Cimoca, Katie Colón, Nancy Condon, Barbara Drewlo, Kerry Dunn, Marti Erding, Sara Freund, Daren Hastings, Ruby Hogen-Chin, Mariann Johanneck, Julie Johnston, Mary Kaye Kuzma, Mary Lukkonen, Carrie O'Connor, Carol Nelson, Marie Schaefle, Julie Theisen, Chris Tures, Mike Vineski, Charmaine Whitman, Sue Will

Copyright © 2009 by Pearson Education, Inc. or its affiliate(s). All rights reserved. Printed in the United States of America. This publication is protected by copyright, and permission should be obtained from the publisher prior to any prohibited reproduction, storage in a retrieval system, or transmission in any form or by any means, electronic, mechanical, photocopying, recording, or likewise. The publisher hereby grants permission to reproduce pages 7–8, 12–13, 17–20, 23–26, 35–36, 40–56, 59–129, 140–143, 167, 168, 178, 181, in part or in whole, for classroom use only, the number not to exceed the number of students in each class. The publisher hereby grants permission to reproduce pages 131–137, 183–192, in part or in whole, for teacher use only. Notice of copyright must appear on all copies. For information regarding permission(s), write to: Pearson School Rights and Permissions Department, One Lake Street, Upper Saddle River, New Jersey 07458.

Pearson® is a trademark, in the U.S. and/or in other countries, of Pearson Education, Inc. or its affiliate(s).

ISBN-13: 978-0-7854-6693-2
ISBN-10:   0-7854-6693-2
1 2 3 4 5 6 7 8 9 10   12 11 10 09 08

1-800-992-0244
www.pearsonschool.com

CONTENTS

What Is *Caught Reading?* v
What Does the *Caught Reading Assessment Manual* Do? vi
Who Is This *Manual* For? vi

Preassessment 1
   Placement 1
      Overview of the Quick Placement Process 3
      Administering the Sample Passage 4
      Administering the Initial Filter 9
      Administering Passages for Levels 4 and 5 14
      Administering the Individual Assessment 21
      Quick Placement Answer Key 27
   Diagnosis 30
      Administering the Elementary Spelling Inventory I 31
      Administering The Names Test of Decoding 34
      Interest Inventory 36

Ongoing Assessment 37
   Administering the Fluency Checks 38
   Fluency Check Answer Keys 57
   Final Assessment for *Getting Ready* 59
   Getting Ready Assessment Checklist 62
   Midway and Final Assessments for Levels 1–7 63
   Administering the High Frequency Words Quizzes 130

Postassessment 138
   Posttest A: Passage 140
   Posttest A: Comprehension Questions 141
   Posttest B: Passage 142
   Posttest B: Comprehension Questions 143
   Posttest Answer Key 144

Reading in Your Classroom 146
   Why Is Reading Assessment Important? 146
   Informal Reading Inventories 148
   Levels of Text Difficulty 149
   An Approach to Reading 152
   The Reading Program 156
   How Do Teachers Manage Multiple Modes? 160
   Five Major Categories of Skill Instruction 162

Assessment Charts 182
    Caught Reading Quick Placement Recording Chart 183
    Student Diagnostic Chart 184
    Error Guide for Elementary Spelling Inventory I 185
    Feature Guide for Elementary Spelling Inventory I 186
    Individual Student Monthly Progress
      Monitoring Chart for *Caught Reading* (Academic Year) 187
    Individual Student Monthly Progress
      Monitoring Chart for *Caught Reading* (Full Calendar Year) 188
    Monthly Class Summary Chart 189
    Fluency Check Student Recording Chart (Levels 1–3) 190
    Fluency Check Student Recording Chart (Levels 4–7) 191
    High Frequency Words Mastery Chart 192

Bibliography 193

What Is *Caught Reading*?

Caught Reading is a comprehensive developmental reading program that helps students who are reading at levels from preliteracy through fourth grade. It is designed to be used with older students—those who have left elementary school without attaining the foundational skills of reading.

The prereading component *(Getting Ready)*, provides basic literacy instruction for these students. It includes explicit instruction in phonemic awareness, the alphabetic principle, and basic phonics, as well as exposure to brief, lively reading selections in many genres, engaging reading-based activities, and opportunities for assessment and reteaching. A few of your secondary students may need to be placed in this program, but most will move on to the developmental reading instruction in *Caught Reading*.

Caught Reading is an eight-level developmental reading program that takes students from a basic literacy to a Grade 4 reading level. Its instructional plan is comprehensive and includes the following strands:

- phonics, decoding, and word attack skills
- spelling activities
- vocabulary development
- fluency (two decodable novels accompany each Level)
- reading comprehension, reading strategies, and literary analysis
- complete assessment program covering three different stages: Preassessment, Ongoing Assessment, and Postassessment
- integration of reading, writing, speaking, and listening
- opportunities for independent reading

Caught Reading Program Components							
	Level 1	**Level 2**	**Level 3**	**Level 4**	**Level 5**	**Level 6**	**Level 7**
Getting Ready Worktext	Worktext 1	Worktext 2	Worktext 3	Worktext 4	Worktext 5	Worktext 6	Worktext 7
	Midway Novel 1	Midway Novel 2	Midway Novel 3	Midway Novel 4	Midway Novel 5	Midway Novel 6	Midway Novel 7
	Final Novel 1	Final Novel 2	Final Novel 3	Final Novel 4	Final Novel 5	Final Novel 6	Final Novel 7
Teacher's Manual							
Assessment Manual							

What Does the *Caught Reading Assessment Manual* Do?

The *Caught Reading Assessment Manual* provides a complete tool for assessing students at three different stages in the program:

Stage I: Preassessment

Stage II: Ongoing Assessment

Stage III: Postassessment

Teachers may use the information they gather from the assessments for both placement and diagnosis.

This *Manual* was developed in response to teachers' needs to place and monitor their students' performance. It is intended to address the basic reading skills in the program: word attack/decoding, spelling, vocabulary development, fluency, and comprehension. The *Manual* also includes background information for teachers in each of these areas, as well as additional activities, games, and graphic organizers for classroom use.

This *Manual* has been developed to help teachers effectively implement *Caught Reading* with their students. Features include:

- Assessment tools to:
    - ■ identify which students need *Caught Reading*.
    - ■ determine accurate placement for each student.
    - ■ analyze the strengths and weaknesses of students in spelling, vocabulary, decoding, comprehension, reading rate, and word recognition.
- Charts to monitor student progress and inform instruction.
- Fluency checks as a tool to monitor reading rate and comprehension.
- High frequency word instruction and activities to build fluency and automaticity, or the ability of the reader to recognize words automatically without hesitation.

Who Is This *Manual* For?

The *Caught Reading Assessment Manual* is intended to be used by teachers who are using *Caught Reading*. It provides diagnostic processes and procedures to help you make informed decisions for student placement in the program, as well as ongoing monitoring of achievement.

The *Caught Reading Assessment Manual* includes three stages of assessment. These stages are Preassessment, Ongoing Assessment, and Postassessment. Each of these stages has been designed to give teachers feedback on student skill development.

PREASSESSMENT

The first section of this book is the Preassessment section. Preassessment is designed to place students within the *Caught Reading* program and diagnose reading skills. The Preassessment section of this *Manual* consists of two distinct parts: Placement and Diagnosis. The following outline shows the two parts and their components:

Preassessment
- **Placement** (pages 1–29)
    - Sample Passage
    - Initial Filter
    - Level Pretests
- **Diagnosis** (pages 30–36)
    - Elementary Spelling Inventory 1
    - Names Test of Decoding
    - Interest Inventory

PLACEMENT

Following is a description of each of the components in the Placement section:

Sample Passage The Sample Passage gives students the opportunity to familiarize themselves with the format of this exam. It allows students to increase their comfort level with the test so that the results of all subsequent tests are an accurate reflection of students' knowledge base. Directions for administering the Sample Passage begin on page 4 of this *Manual*. The Sample Passage is located on pages 7–8 of this *Manual*.

Initial Filter The Initial Filter determines whether students are ready to enter the *Caught Reading* program. The test is administered to the whole class. Students read the passage silently and respond to comprehension questions as directed. The Initial Filter allows you to quickly determine whether students are candidates for placement within the *Caught Reading* program. Directions for administering the Initial Filter begin on page 9 of this *Manual*. The Initial Filter is located on pages 12–13 of this *Manual*.

Level Pretests The Level Pretests determine where students should be placed in *Caught Reading* and identify their reading comprehension skills. These tests are administered to the whole class. Students read the passages silently and respond to comprehension questions as directed. Directions for administering the Level Pretests begin on page 14 of this *Manual*. The Level Pretests are located on pages 17–20 of this *Manual*. Student data can be recorded in the *Caught Reading* Quick Placement Recording Chart located on page 183 of this *Manual*. The Student Diagnostic Chart on page 184 of this *Manual* can help monitor students' progress.

Instructional Levels

Student reading abilities fall into three main categories, as outlined in the chart below. It is important for students to be placed into materials at their **instructional level**. This placement ensures that they can have successful experiences and can learn and apply new reading strategies. The assessment in this booklet will aid teachers in appropriately placing their students.

INDEPENDENT LEVEL	INSTRUCTIONAL LEVEL	FRUSTRATION LEVEL
The Reader:	The Reader:	The Reader:
decodes with 95-99% accuracy*	decodes with 90–95% accuracy	decodes with less than 90% accuracy
comprehends with 95-99% accuracy	comprehends with at least 75% accuracy	comprehends with less than 50% accuracy
reads with little effort	uses effective strategies to comprehend text	has no strategies to comprehend text
has necessary background information, experiences, and interest	has limited background information, experiences, and interest	has little or no background information, experiences, or interest
has a good grasp of language and vocabulary usage	needs some assistance with vocabulary and language usage	needs to have the material read aloud by another reader/tape
reads without outside assistance	needs some teacher guidance during reading	requires full assistance of teacher, much scaffolding/discussion
makes connections to own life and experiences; metacognition	makes literal interpretation; makes limited connections to own life and experiences	needs specific interpretation of text; needs encouragement and support

There is another stage that can be referred to as the Instructional/Frustration Level. This gray area represents students who comprehend with between 76 percent and 94 percent accuracy. Their comprehension is dependent upon any criteria that might cause them to expend great effort to decode or comprehend difficult material. These criteria might include students' interest level, background knowledge, or a desire to please the teacher.

*It is interesting to note that the Independent Level represents students decoding at a maximum of 99 percent accuracy, instead of 100 percent. This is because even the most competent readers can miscue on something in the text because they anticipate something different or because they simply get distracted.

Overview of the Quick Placement Process

DAY 1 (One class period)
For all students

STEP 1: Administer and Score Sample Passage	STEP 2: Administer Initial Filter	STEP 3: Evaluate Scores for Initial Filter
• Whole class administration • Use Sample Passage to help students understand assessment process. • Students read passage silently and respond to comprehension questions independently. • Students self-score and discuss process with teacher. • Use answer key on page 27 of this *Manual*.	• Whole class administration • Students read Initial Filter silently and respond to comprehension questions independently. • If desired, students can self-correct multiple choice responses.	• Use answer key on page 27 of this *Manual*. • Students who score **90–100%** (miss 0-1): begin instruction in *Be A Better Reader: Level A*. If answers are complete but lacking in depth, consider *Be A Better Reader: Starting Out*. • Students who score **below 90%** (miss more than 1): continue with the *Caught Reading* assessment.

DAY 2 (One class period)
For placement in the *Caught Reading* program
(those who scored below 90% on Initial Filter)

STEP 1: Administer Passages for Levels 4 and 5	STEP 2: Evaluate Scores for Levels 4 and 5	STEP 3: Begin Instruction
• Administer passages for Levels 4 and 5 in the same whole class manner as the Initial Filter. • Score both sets of responses, add the two scores together, and calculate a percent-correct score, i.e., 16 correct out of 20 is 80%. • Use answer key on page 28 of this *Manual*.	**90–100%** (miss 0–2 questions on both tests) ⇓ Place in **Level 6** **75–85%** (miss 3–5 questions on both tests) ⇓ Place in **Level 5** **55–70%** (miss 6–9 questions on both tests) ⇓ Place in **Level 4** **50% or less** (miss 10 or more questions on both tests) ⇓ **Assess individually** (see instructions)	Begin instruction in *Caught Reading*.

Administering the Sample Passage (30 minutes)

About the Sample Passage

The purpose of the Sample Passage is to help students understand and feel comfortable with the assessment process. The passage is administered on a whole class basis. Students read the passage silently and respond to comprehension questions in writing. The Sample Passage can be found on pages 7–8 of this *Manual*.

Directions

1. Before administering the Sample Passage...

Take a few minutes to lay the groundwork for the assessment, helping students understand its seriousness and importance. Include these points:

- Students will be participating in an assessment process that will help teachers determine which materials to use to help them increase their reading skills.

- It is important that they do their best. The results of this assessment will have a long-term effect on their classroom instruction.

- Their answers will not be scored for a grade but will be used to decide which book they will use in their reading class.

- For the first part of the assessment, students will all be reading the same two passages.

- The first passage, or the sample passage, is used to help students feel comfortable with the assessment process. Students will read it in the same manner as the official passages but will self-score and discuss the answering process.

- The second passage, or the Initial Filter, will be the official assessment, and the results will be used to determine the need for further assessment.

2. Administer the Sample Passage.

- Students may read the passage as many times as needed to become familiar with it.
- When students finish reading, they will answer 10 questions about the passage.
- The passage will be removed before students are given the questions.

    Note: It is important to emphasize this point repeatedly, encouraging students to read the passage several times. They may not understand that they need to remember the information without having the passage in front of them for reference.

- Students will respond to the comprehension questions on page 8 of this *Manual*. Some questions are multiple choice and some are open-ended, requiring students to write out their answers.
- Students do not have to answer the open-ended questions in complete sentences, and spelling errors will not lower their grades. However, they should do their best in those areas, as well as write neatly, so their answers can be read easily.
- They should keep the answers to the open-ended items (Questions 7–10) brief but complete and based on what they read in the text.
- There are no time limits for reading the passage or answering the questions.
- The answers to some of the questions may not be directly stated in the passage.

3. Have students read the Sample Passage and answer the comprehension questions.

- As individual students finish reading the passage, collect it and distribute the comprehension question sheet.
- Students mark their answers to the 10 comprehension questions directly on the sheet. Be sure their names and the date are on their papers.

4. Score the Sample Passage.

When all students are finished, have them trade papers and score the answers. For the open-ended questions, provide suggested answers and help them evaluate the responses. Answers can be found on page 27 of this *Manual*.

Discuss the process with students. Here are a few guidelines:

- Which kinds of questions did they miss?
  Questions 1–5 are direct recall; answers must be as stated in the passage.
  Question 6 is vocabulary.
  Question 7 is the topic or a short title of the passage.
  Questions 8–9 are inference.
  Question 10 is evaluation.

- Which questions were hardest for them?

- What could they do differently to help them on the official test?
  Sometimes students tend to read the passage too quickly and begin work on the comprehension questions without fully understanding the passage. As part of this discussion, help them to realize the importance of rereading the passage to improve their comprehension.

- Transition to the Initial Filter, reminding students to think about this discussion as they read it.

SAMPLE: Passage

DIRECTIONS: Read the passage below. You may read it as many times as you need to for complete understanding. When you are finished, raise your hand, and the teacher will bring you a set of questions to answer. Remember, you will not have the passage when answering the questions.

Over the roar of the fire, Tom heard John shout, "Hurry! The fire is almost on us!"

Tom's arms were sore and tired, but he swung his axe even faster. He didn't even stop to wipe the tears from his stinging eyes. The greedy fire kept coming. The more the fire destroyed, the more it wanted. Tom worked shoulder to shoulder with the other smoke jumpers. His only thought was to stop the flaming monster that was raging through the forest.

At last the smoke jumpers finished the firebreak. If the fire was powerful enough, it would jump over the firebreak that they had worked so hard to make. Then they would have to start all over again.

Tom stood motionless, his face black with ash, his shirt wet with sweat. He was too exhausted to move. He had given all of himself to fighting the fire. He turned his head and noticed John watching him. John nodded.

Suddenly all that John had taught Tom about proving his bravery was clear. A man was not brave if he did something just to prove his courage. He was brave only when he forgot about himself. Today Tom had showed that he cared very much about the others with whom he was working.

Name _____ Date _____

SAMPLE: Comprehension Questions

Directions: Circle the correct answer for Questions 1–6. This is not a timed test.

1. It was hard for Tom to do his job because
    a. his arms were sore and tired.
    b. he couldn't think very well.
    c. he worked shoulder to shoulder with other smoke jumpers.

2. Tom's only thought as he tried to put out the fire was
    a. to get some rest.
    b. to get something to drink.
    c. to stop the flaming monster.

3. To try and stop the fire from spreading, the smoke jumpers built a
    a. firebreak.
    b. fire.
    c. water line.

4. Tom had given so much to fight the fire that he
    a. turned his head to look at John.
    b. was too exhausted to move.
    c. was black with ash.

5. John taught Tom that being brave
    a. comes from working very hard.
    b. comes from doing something to prove your courage.
    c. comes from forgetting about yourself.

6. What does *greedy* mean in this sentence from the passage: "The <u>greedy</u> fire kept coming."
    a. wanting less
    b. wanting more
    c. wanting to move

Directions: For Questions 7–10, you must write out your answer. Spelling and punctuation will not be graded, but you should do your best.

7. What is this passage mostly about? _____
_____
_____

8. What do you think the firefighters used to build the firebreak? _____
_____
_____

9. Why do you think John nodded when he was watching Tom? _____
_____
_____

10. How would you act if you had to fight a fire like Tom did? Why? _____
_____
_____

Administering the Initial Filter (20 minutes)

About the Initial Filter

The purpose of the Initial Filter in the placement process is to show which students are ready to progress to *Be A Better Reader: Level A* and which students need to work in the *Caught Reading* program. The passage is administered on a whole class basis. Students read the passages silently and respond to comprehension questions in writing. The Initial Filter can be found on pages 12–13 of this *Manual*.

Directions

1. **Before administering the Initial Filter...**

   Remind students about the discussion points from the Sample Passage.

2. **Administer the Initial Filter.**

   If necessary, repeat the directions for the Sample Passage.

   - Students may read the passage as many times as needed to become familiar with it.

   - When students finish reading, they will answer 10 questions about the passage.

   - The passage will be removed before students are given the questions.

     Note: It is important to emphasize this point repeatedly, encouraging students to read the passage several times. They may not understand that they need to remember the information without having the passage in front of them for reference.

   - Students will respond to the comprehension questions on page 13 of this *Manual*. Some questions are multiple choice and some are open-ended, requiring students to write out their answers.

   - Students do not have to answer the open-ended questions in complete sentences, and spelling errors will not lower their grades. However, they should do their best in those areas, as well as write neatly so their answers can be read easily.

   - They should keep the answers to the open-ended items (Questions 7–10) brief but complete and based on what they read in the text.

   - There are no time limits for reading the passage or answering the questions.

   - The answers to some of the questions may not be directly stated in the passage.

3. Have students read the passage and answer the comprehension questions.

- As individual students finish reading the passage, collect it and distribute the comprehension question sheet.
- Students mark their answers to the 10 comprehension questions directly on the sheet. Be sure their names and the date are on their papers.

4. After students complete the assessment...

When finished with the passage and questions, students may quietly occupy themselves until all of them are finished.

Observe student behavior during the assessment. The following behaviors may signal serious reading difficulties.

- Student takes an excessive amount of time to read the passage.
- Student reads the passage very quickly, but then does poorly on the questions.
- Student exhibits signs of excessive physical discomfort during the reading.
- Student uses delaying tactics to avoid reading completely.

Quietly take aside any student who exhibits any of these behaviors, and ask if he or she is having problems. At this point, it would be appropriate to have the student read the passage aloud. If, during this informal assessment, the student demonstrates extreme difficulty with recognition, make an immediate correction in the assessment process and move to the Individual Assessment, which begins on page 21 of this *Manual*.

5. Score the Initial Filter.

Use the answer key for the Initial Filter on page 27 of this *Manual* to determine the number of correct answers for each student.

- Questions 1–5 are recall with multiple-choice responses.
- Question 6 is vocabulary, also multiple choice.
- The response for Question 7 must be a short phrase, or possibly one word, that summarizes the passage. Suggested answers are given for your reference.
- For inferential items (Questions 8–9) and the evaluative item (Question 10), students' responses must relate to the information in the passage and must add ideas and information from their own thoughts, supported by appropriate reasoning. To be completely correct, the answer must include a response to the "Why or why not?" portion of the question. Half credit may be given for an answer that gives a good response to the first part but does not explain why the response was given.

To determine placement for your students, use the chart below. If students score:

90% or Better	Less than 90%
⇩	⇩
move to *Be A Better Reader: Level A*.	continue with the *Caught Reading* assessment process as described on the following pages.
Students should have received 90% or better and have full, complete answers for Questions 7–10. If their answers are correct, but lacking in depth, you may want to consider placement in *Be A Better Reader: Starting Out* or Level 6 of *Caught Reading*.	These students will have missed more than one question.

Record student scores on the *Caught Reading* Quick Placement Recording Chart on page 183 of this *Manual* to facilitate ease of ordering and selecting materials.

INITIAL FILTER: Passage

Directions: Read the passage below. You may read it as many times as you need to for complete understanding. When you are finished, raise your hand, and the teacher will bring you a set of questions to answer. Remember, you will not have the passage when answering the questions.

Veterinarians weren't always around. In fact, the first veterinary schools weren't started until the late 1700s. Before that time, animals were cared for by the people who worked with them—shepherds, farmers, stable hands, and others. These people depended on their experience and sometimes folk wisdom, rather than science, to treat their animals.

The first trained veterinarians generally treated only large animals, such as cows, horses, sheep, goats, and pigs. These animals were very important in a farm-based economy. Vets who specialized in treating small animals, mainly pets, were unheard of at that time. But then cities grew, and society and the economy changed. More people started to own pets. Gradually, more and more veterinarians began setting up small-animal practices.

Today, Dr. Wendell Jordan and veterinarians like him who work in small towns and rural areas usually have a mixed practice. These country vets still treat horses and livestock, such as dairy cows and pigs, but they also treat wildlife and pets. Dr. Jordan usually spends the morning in his office taking care of pet cats and dogs that need checkups, shots, or medicine. Sometimes, however, a small patient turns out to be a wild animal like an injured fawn.

Once Dr. Jordan leaves his office, his examining room or operating room may be a pasture or a barn stall. Equipment has to be portable, small enough to be carried in a truck or van. He does not have a laboratory with him that can do tests.

That's not to say that a city vet's practice is dull. People living in cities often have exotic pets. Dr. Catherine Ling, an urban vet, sometimes sees in her city practice such unusual patients as chameleons, parrots, ferrets, and snakes.

Like many other city veterinarians, Dr. Ling works with a team of vets in a clinic. Generally, these clinics are equipped like human hospitals. Working in teams is helpful because the vets can see a greater number and variety of patients.

Name _____ Date _____

INITIAL FILTER: Comprehension Questions

Directions: Circle the correct answer for Questions 1–6. This is not a timed test.

1. The first schools for veterinarians started in the
   a. early 1700s.
   b. 1800s.
   c. late 1700s.

2. Two kinds of people who cared for animals before there were trained vets were
   a. housewives and children.
   b. shepherds and farmers.
   c. families and doctors.

3. Two animals that the first trained vets generally treated were
   a. cows and sheep.
   b. dogs and sheep.
   c. horses and cats.

4. The workplaces are different for the country vet and the urban vet because
   a. Dr. Jordan works in his office, and Dr. Ling works in a hospital.
   b. Dr. Jordan leaves his office, and Dr. Ling stays in her clinic.
   c. Dr. Jordan works in a truck, and Dr. Ling works in a clinic.

5. A city vet might treat
   a. chameleons and snakes.
   b. tigers and parrots.
   c. snakes and monkeys.

6. What does *urban* mean in this sentence from the passage: "Dr. Catherine Ling, an <u>urban</u> vet…"
   a. country
   b. suburban
   c. city

Directions: For Questions 7–10, you must write out your answer. Spelling and punctuation will not be graded, but you should do your best.

7. What is this passage mostly about? _____
_____
_____

8. Why do you think people start owning pets? _____
_____
_____

9. Do you think it is important to take care of animals? _____
   Why or why not? _____
   _____

10. If you were a vet, where would you like to work? _____
    Explain your answer. _____
    _____

13

Administering Passages for Levels 4 and 5 (20–30 minutes)

About the Passages

These passages are administered to students who scored **below 90 percent** on the Initial Filter. The passages are drawn from the *Caught Reading* program. They are designed to serve as a quick assessment tool for effectively placing students in the *Caught Reading* program. The passages are administered on a whole class basis. Students read the passages silently and respond to comprehension questions in writing. These passages can be found on pages 17–20 of this *Manual*.

Directions

1. **Before administering the Level 4 Passage...**

   Remind students about the discussion points from the Sample Passage.

2. **Administer the Level 4 Passage.**

   If necessary, repeat the directions for the Sample Passage:

   - Students may read each passage as many times as needed in order to be familiar with it.

   - When students finish reading, they will answer 10 questions about the passage.

   - The passage will be removed before students are given the questions.

     Note: It is important to emphasize this point repeatedly, encouraging students to read the passage several times. They may not understand that they need to remember the information without having the passage in front of them for reference.

   - Students will respond to the comprehension questions on page 18 of this *Manual*. Some questions are multiple choice, and some are open-ended, requiring students to write out their answers.

   - Students do not have to answer the open-ended questions in complete sentences, and spelling errors will not lower their grades. However, they should do their best in those areas, as well as write neatly so their answers can be read easily.

   - They should keep the answers to the open-ended items (Questions 7–10) brief but complete and based on what they read in the text.

   - There are no time limits for reading the passage or answering the questions.

   - The answers to some of the questions may not be directly stated in the passage.

3. Have students read the Level 4 Passage and answer the comprehension questions.

- As individual students finish reading the passage, collect it and distribute the comprehension question sheet.
- Students mark their answers to the 10 comprehension questions directly on the sheet. Be sure their names and the date are on their papers.

4. Administer the Level 5 Passage.

- As individual students finish with the comprehension questions for Level 4, collect it and distribute the passage for Level 5.

5. Have students read the Level 5 Passage and answer the comprehension questions.

- As individual students finish reading the passage, collect it and distribute a copy of the comprehension questions located on page 20 of this *Manual*.
- Students mark their answers to the 10 comprehension questions directly on the sheet. Be sure their names and the date are on their papers.

6. After students complete the assessment...

When finished with the passage and questions, students may quietly occupy themselves until all of them are finished.

Observe student behavior during the assessment. The following behaviors may signal serious reading difficulties.

- Student takes an excessive amount of time to read the passage.
- Student reads the passage very quickly, but then does poorly on the questions.
- Student exhibits signs of excessive physical discomfort during the reading.
- Student uses delaying tactics to avoid reading completely.

Quietly take aside any student who exhibits any of these behaviors, and ask if he or she is having problems. At this point, it would be appropriate to have the student read the passage aloud. If, during this informal assessment, the student demonstrates extreme difficulty with recognition, make an immediate correction in the assessment process, and move to the Individual Assessment, which begins on page 21 of this *Manual*.

7. Evaluate scores for the Levels 4 and 5 Passages.

Use the answer key on page 28 of this *Manual* to determine the number of correct answers for each student.

- Questions 1–5 are recall with multiple-choice responses.
- Question 6 is vocabulary, also multiple choice.
- The response for Question 7 must be a short phrase, or possibly one word, that summarizes the passage. Suggested answers are given for your reference.
- For inferential items (Questions 8–9) and the evaluative item (Question 10), students' responses must relate to the information in the passage and must add ideas and information from their own thoughts, supported by appropriate reasoning. Students can earn 10 percent for each correct answer. However, the percentages shown in the chart on this page are in 5 percent increments because students can receive half credit, or 5 percent, for an open-ended question. To be completely correct, the answer must include a response to the "Why or why not?" portion of the question. Half credit may be given for an answer that gives a good response to the first part, but does not explain why the response was given.

To determine placement for each student, add the scores for both passages and calculate a percent-correct score. For example, 16 correct out of 20 is 80 percent. Use the chart below for placement or further testing. Students whose score averages:

Less than 50%	55–70%	75–85%	90–100%
(missed 10+ questions on both tests) ⇓ Place in **Level 3**. or Administer **Individual Assessment** (see page 21) Passages 4 and 5 are written at the second and third grade level. Students who still do not show instructional-level comprehension need further diagnosis.	(missed 6–9 questions on both tests) ⇓ Place in **Level 4**.	(missed 3–5 questions on both tests) ⇓ Place in **Level 5**.	(missed 0–2 questions on both tests) ⇓ Place in **Level 6**.

Note: If teachers have more than one or two Levels in each classroom, consider placing all students who score 75 percent or higher in the level at which the majority scored. Allow for instructional pacing as needed.

Record student scores on the Quick Placement Recording Chart on page 183 of this Manual to facilitate ease of ordering and selecting materials.

8. Begin instruction.

Begin instruction in the appropriate level of *Caught Reading*.

LEVEL 4: Passage

Directions: Read the passage below. You may read it as many times as you need to for complete understanding. When you are finished, raise your hand, and the teacher will bring you a set of questions to answer. Remember, you will not have the passage when answering the questions.

The biggest fish in the sea is the shark. But when most people think of sharks, they don't think big. They think monster. Why are people scared? Look into the mouth of one, and you'll see why.

A shark has many lines of teeth. When its mouth is closed, its teeth point to the back. But when the mouth opens, all the teeth point to the front. Sharks never run out of teeth. As the front teeth wear down, they fall out. The next line of teeth then moves to the front. A shark gets a new line of teeth every one to two weeks.

Most sharks live on fish. But they will eat any animal they can find. In fact, sharks may even take in things that are not alive. One shark had a bike inside it when it was caught and cut open!

It is hard to get away from a shark in the water. For one thing, sharks can see really well. Their eyes do not need much light. In fact, sharks see best after the sun goes down.

Sharks can get around even in the darkest night. They don't need to see to find animals. They can do this without using their eyes. When a fish goes through the water, it makes the water move. Sharks can tell what is making the water move and where the fish is. So even if a fish is hiding, a shark can find it.

Sharks cannot stop moving. If they stop moving, they die. So even in their sleep, sharks keep moving. Sharks circle a fish before they attack it. At first, they make a big circle. Then they move in, going even faster. At last, they turn in and hit the fish.

Many sharks have a little fish that goes with them everywhere. The little fish works for the shark. It keeps the shark clean. The shark does not attack this little fish.

Now and again, you hear about a shark that attacks people. Scientists do not know why sharks at times attack people and at other times leave them be.

Name _____ Date _____

LEVEL 4: Comprehension Questions

Directions: Circle the correct answer for Questions 1–6. This is not a timed test.

1. When most people think of a shark, they think of
   a. a mouth.
   b. a monster.
   c. something big.

2. When a shark's front teeth wear down, they
   a. fall out.
   b. get sharper.
   c. run out.

3. When one shark was caught and cut open, someone found a
   a. bike.
   b. tire.
   c. human.

4. It is hard to get away from a shark in the water because a shark
   a. hides.
   b. is too big.
   c. sees really well.

5. If a shark stops moving, it
   a. sleeps.
   b. dies.
   c. circles a fish.

6. What does *circle* mean in this sentence from the passage: "Sharks circle a fish before they attack it."
   a. make a ring around
   b. draw a circle
   c. move forward

Directions: For Questions 7–10, you must write out your answer. Spelling and punctuation will not be graded, but you should do your best.

7. What is this passage mostly about? _____
_____
_____

8. Why do you think sharks need new teeth every one to two weeks? _____
_____
_____

9. Why might a shark try to eat something that is not alive? _____
_____
_____

10. What would you do if you saw a shark attacking someone? _____
    Explain your answer. _____
_____
_____

LEVEL 5: Passage

Directions: Read the passage below. You may read it as many times as you need to for complete understanding. When you are finished, raise your hand, and the teacher will bring you a set of questions to answer. Remember, you will not have the passage when answering the questions.

Wilma Mankiller was the principal chief of the Cherokee nation. She was the first woman to be chief. She was born in 1945 in a small Oklahoma town.

When she was 11, her family moved to California. In 1972, she started college. However, she did not finish college. In 1976, she went home to her small town in Oklahoma. She could not find any work there. So back she went to California. Then she went back again to her small town. Wilma was having problems getting her life together. This time, she stayed in Oklahoma. She got a job working for the Cherokee nation. She went back to school, too. In 1979, she finished college.

Then she went on to even more school. Wilma was starting to find out who she was and what she wanted to do with her life. She was thinking a lot about the Cherokee people. Some were so poor that they did not have water for farming or to use in their homes. She had an idea about building a water pipeline. But she didn't know how to go about doing it.

Then Wilma was in a bad car accident. She almost died. This changed the way she looked at life. She now knew that she wanted to give her life to making things better for the Cherokee nation.

Today, Wilma talks of the "woman who lived before and the woman who lived after" the car accident. The woman who lived before didn't know what she wanted. The woman who lived after was ready to become chief of the Cherokee nation.

Name _____ Date _____

LEVEL 5: Comprehension Questions

Directions: Circle the correct answer for Questions 1–6. This is not a timed test.

1. The two states in which Wilma lived were
    a. Wyoming and California.
    b. California and Oklahoma.
    c. California and Cherokee.

2. She finally finished college in
    a. 1997.
    b. 1979.
    c. 1945.

3. Some of the Cherokee people were so poor that they did not
    a. have schools.
    b. have enough food to eat.
    c. have water for farming or for their homes.

4. Wilma wanted to help the Cherokee people by
    a. building a water pipeline.
    b. teaching them about farming.
    c. giving them money.

5. Wilma changed the way she looked at life after she
    a. went back to school.
    b. almost died in a car accident.
    c. became the chief.

6. What does *nation* mean in this sentence from the passage: "She got a job working for the Cherokee nation."
    a. group of people who live together
    b. government
    c. a town in Oklahoma

Directions: For Questions 7–10, you must write out your answer. Spelling and punctuation will not be graded, but you should do your best.

7. What is this passage mostly about? _____
   _____
   _____

8. Why do you think Wilma had a hard time getting her life together? _____
   _____
   _____

9. What do you think Wilma meant when she talked of the "woman who lived before and the woman who lived after?" _____
   _____
   _____

10. Do you think Wilma was a successful chief of the Cherokee nation? _____
    Explain your answer. _____
    _____

Administering the Individual Assessment

About Individual Assessment

Individual Assessment may be used in either of the following two situations:

- Student scores **50 percent or less** on combined scores on passages for Levels 4 and 5.
- Student exhibits the following during assessment, such as:
  1. taking an excessive amount of time to read the passage.
  2. reading the passage very quickly, but then doing poorly on the comprehension questions.
  3. showing signs of excessive physical discomfort during the reading.
  4. using delaying tactics to avoid reading completely.

Directions

1. Before administering the Level 4 Passage...

Take a few minutes to lay the groundwork for the assessment, helping the student understand the process.

- Remind the student that he/she has already read the passage for Level 4 during the whole class administration.
- First, the student will read the passage aloud to the teacher.
- Then, the teacher will take the passage away and ask the student questions about the passage.

2. Administer the Level 4 Passage.

- Have the student read the passage orally while you mark decoding errors on your copy of the Level 4 Passage. You may use the chart on this page for marking word recognition errors, or you may use any other markings to suit your needs. The same error made consistently throughout a passage counts as one error. An entire line omitted and not corrected is one error.

TRACKING DECODING ERRORS	
Decoding Error	**Mark**
Student reads text accurately	no mark
Substitution for correct word	attempted word actual word in text
Student makes no attempt at word; teacher supplies word	T over text
Student omits word	X over text
Student adds word to text	insertion text^text
Student repeats text	R over text
Student self-corrects an error	attempted word/sc over text

3. Ask the comprehension questions.
- Read the comprehension questions for the passage aloud to the student.
- Record the student's responses directly on the comprehension question sheet.

4. Evaluate responses and determine placement.
Use the answer key on page 28 of this *Manual* to evaluate your students' responses and determine placement using the chart below. You will see one of the following four results:

Result 1	Result 2	Result 3	Result 4
The student will decode fluently, but will still not be able to answer the questions or tell you what the passage is about.	The student will decode fairly accurately, but slowly, drawing out the words in a manner that indicates the focus is centered on decoding and there is a lack of automaticity.	The student will not be able to decode at a 90% proficiency level, but will be able to answer the comprehension questions with at least 70% accuracy, perhaps because the second reading helped or there is adequate background knowledge.	The student will neither be able to decode at an instructional level nor answer at least 70% of the comprehension questions, even on this second reading.
⇓	⇓	⇓	⇓
Continue with the oral reading for several more passages to see if this is the main problem. If so, place in **Level 4** with the awareness that explicit teaching of comprehension strategies will be necessary.	Place in **Level 4**. Emphasize high frequency words and fluency strategies.	Administer the passages for **Levels 2 and 3** to analyze decoding issues. If the student still demonstrates decoding difficulty, consider *Getting Ready,* or begin in **Level 1**.	Administer the passages for **Levels 2 and 3**. Repeat the process and place as scores indicate. If the student still demonstrates decoding difficulties, consider *Getting Ready,* or begin in **Level 1**.

LEVEL 2: Passage for Individual Assessment

Directions: Read the passage below. You may read it as many times as you need to for complete understanding. When you are ready, raise your hand. Then, read the passage aloud to your teacher. When you are finished, your teacher will remove the passage and give you a set of questions to answer. Remember, you will not have the passage when answering the questions.

One day as I was walking to school, Jared said, "Did you hear about the bank window?"

"No," I said.

"It was smashed by a baseball, and I am going to tell the bank who did it. That family should not be sleeping in that field."

I feel sick. It was not right for that family to smash the bank window. But Jared does not have to tell on the family.

The next day I see Jared. "Did you tell the people at the bank?" I asked.

"Yes, I did," Jared answered.

"And?"

"The family already talked to the bank and paid for the window," said Jared. "Just like they should have."

"Where did homeless people get money for a window?" I asked.

"Not my problem," he says.

That night, I take a hot dinner to the field. The man will not talk to me. But the woman takes the hot dinner and gives it to her little boy.

"Did you come to find out about the bank window? My boy was playing with the baseball. He didn't mean to break the window."

"What do you want?" the man says to me. "What are you doing here?"

The woman says, "He is mad because the money we gave to the bank was going to pay for an apartment. Now we have to start over."

"Do you have jobs?" I ask.

"He does," the woman tells me, "but I don't. It takes a long time to save enough money for an apartment."

I can just hear Jared saying, "Not my problem." But it feels like a problem. I don't think people should have to sleep in a field in the cold.

Name _____ Date _____

LEVEL 2: Comprehension Questions

Directions: Circle the correct answer for Questions 1–6. This is not a timed test.

1. The bank window was smashed by
   a. some boys.
   b. a baseball.
   c. a car.

2. Jared wants to tell the bank who broke the window because
   a. he thinks the family should not be living in the field.
   b. he is mad.
   c. his father works at the bank.

3. The people at the bank find out who broke the window because
   a. the family tells them.
   b. Jared tells them.
   c. a police officer tells them.

4. The family was planning to use the money to
   a. buy food.
   b. buy clothes.
   c. pay for an apartment.

5. Only one of the parents has
   a. a car.
   b. a job.
   c. food.

6. What does *problem* mean in this sentence from the passage: "Not my problem."
   a. something easy to do
   b. something to worry about
   c. something sad

Directions. For Questions 7–10, you must write out your answers. Spelling and punctuation will not be graded, but you should do your best.

7. What is this passage mostly about? _____
   _____
   _____

8. Why does Jared's friend say, "I can just hear Jared saying, 'Not my problem?'"
   _____
   _____
   _____

9. Why do you think Jared's friend took a hot dinner to the family? _____
   _____
   _____

10. What would you have done to help the family if you were there? _____
    Explain your answer. _____
    _____
    _____

LEVEL 3: Passage for Individual Assessment

Directions: Read the passage below. You may read it as many times as you need to for complete understanding. When you are ready, raise your hand. Then, read the passage aloud to your teacher. When you are finished, your teacher will remove the passage and give you a set of questions to answer. Remember, you will not have the passage when answering the questions.

Carmen and Tom are walking by some shops. Carmen stops.

"Look over there."

Tom sees a boy writing on the wall.

"Wait here," says Carmen. She goes over to the boy and asks, "What are you doing?"

"I am writing an ad. What does it look like?"

"An ad for what?" asks Carmen.

"An ad for myself," says the boy. "Who else?"

"On a wall?" asks Carmen.

"That's the point!" the boy says. "I want lots of people to see it." He goes on working. "There! That's that. What do you think? Move back a little. That way you can see it better."

Carmen looks up. She sees the ad. The letters are as big as people. She reads the words. They say: "Luis is the man. Luis is the best. What a hot guy!"

"Are you Luis?" she asks.

"Yes, I am." His face lights up. "I am the man himself. Luis is my name. Writing on walls is my game. I have what it takes and it shows. Who are you?"

"I'm Carmen," she says. "I think I am going to be sick."

"Many people have these feelings at first," Luis tells her. "You will get over it. Already I think you like me. Don't try to hide it. I know people, and I can always tell. So what do you say? Let's go out someday."

Carmen looks Luis over. She says, "How about today?"

"Man! You don't play games, do you? I like that," says Luis. "I have a lot of girls after me, but I like you best. Really. Where should we go?"

"I know just the place," says Carmen. She starts for the school.

Name _____ Date _____

LEVEL 3: Comprehension Questions

Directions: Circle the correct answer for Questions 1–6. This is not a timed test.

1. The boy tells Carmen that he is
   a. writing on the wall.
   b. writing an ad for himself.
   c. looking for a job.

2. The boy tells Carmen to
   a. move back so she can see better.
   b. write an ad.
   c. look up.

3. One sentence Luis writes is
   a. "Luis is cool."
   b. "Luis is the man."
   c. "Luis is big and tall."

4. When Carmen tells Luis she thinks she is going to be sick, Luis says,
   a. "I'm sorry."
   b. "Most people like me."
   c. "Many people have these feelings at first."

5. When Luis asks her to go out someday, Carmen says,
   a. "How about today?"
   b. "I don't have time."
   c. "I don't like you."

6. What does *game* means in this sentence from the passage: "Writing on walls is my game."
   a. how he plays basketball
   b. what he does
   c. how to play cards

Directions: For Questions 7–10, you must write out your answer. Spelling and punctuation will not be graded, but you should do your best.

7. What is this passage mostly about? _____

8. Why do you think Carmen is taking Luis to the school? _____

9. How do you think Luis feels about himself? Why? _____

10. What would you do if you were Carmen and you saw someone writing on a wall? Explain your answer. _____

Quick Placement Answer Key

Sample Passage
Recall
1. a   2. c   3. a   4. b   5. c.

Vocabulary
6. b

Topic/Title
7. What is this passage mostly about? *smoke jumpers fighting a fire*

Inference
8. What do you think the firefighters used to build the firebreak? *They chopped down trees or dug out a wide space in the forest, so the fire wouldn't have anything to burn.*

9. Why do you think John nodded when he was watching Tom? *Accept any logical response: to show Tom he had done a good job; that John approved of Tom's actions; that Tom had been brave, as John taught him to be.*

Evaluation
10. How would you act if you had to fight a fire like Tom did? Why? *Accept any logical response supported with appropriate reasons.*

Initial Filter
Recall
1. c   2. b   3. a   4. b   5. a

Vocabulary
6. c

Topic/Title
7. What is this passage mostly about? *veterinarians*

Inference
8. Why do you think people start owning pets? *Accept any logical response that relates to more money: more leisure time; the fact that people lived in cities and not on farms.*

9. Do you think it is important to take care of animals? Why or why not? *Accept any logical response: People love their pets; animals are used for food, work, and so on.*

Evaluation
10. If you were a vet, where would you like to work? Explain your answer. *Accept any logical response supported with appropriate reasons.*

Quick Placement Answer Key (Continued)

Level 4 Passage

Recall

1. b   2. a   3. a   4. c   5. b

Vocabulary

6. a

Topic/Title

7. What is this passage mostly about? *sharks and how they live*

Inference

8. Why do you think sharks need new teeth every one to two weeks? *Accept any logical response relating to eating so many different things: the teeth wear down and fall out.*

9. Why might a shark try to eat something that is not alive? *Accept any logical response relating to a shark grabbing anything that is in the water or needing a lot to eat.*

Evaluation

10. What would you do if you saw a shark attacking someone? Explain your answer. *Accept any logical response that is supported by reasoning.*

Level 5 Passage

Recall

1. b   2. b   3. c   4. a   5. b

Vocabulary

6. a

Topic/Title

7. What is this passage mostly about? *Wilma Mankiller and her life; how Wilma's life was changed*

Inference

8. Why do you think Wilma had a hard time getting her life together? *Accept any logical response relating to parents, small-town life, personal problems, couldn't find work.*

9. What do you think Wilma meant when she talked of the "woman who lived before and the woman who lived after?" *Her life was changed by the accident; she became a different person; she had a purpose in life.*

Evaluation

10. Do you think Wilma was a successful chief of the Cherokee nation? Explain your answer. *Accept any logical response: Her life was changed; she knew what she wanted; she cares about the Cherokee nation.*

Quick Placement Answer Key (Continued)

Level 2 Passage

Recall

1. b   2. a   3. a   4. c   5. b

Vocabulary

6. b

Topic/Title

7. What is this passage mostly about? *a bank window that is broken; a family that has a problem*

Inference

8. Why does Jared's friend say, "I can just hear Jared saying, 'Not my problem?'" *Because Jared wouldn't be concerned about the people; he didn't care about them.*

9. Why do you think Jared's friend took a hot dinner to the family? *Accept any logical response relating to the friend worrying about the family and wanting to help.*

Evaluation

10. What would you have done to help the family if you were there? Explain your answer. *Accept any logical response supported with appropriate reasons.*

Level 3 Passage

Recall

1. b   2. a   3. b   4. c   5. a

Vocabulary

6. b

Topic/Title

7. What is this passage mostly about? *a boy writing on a wall*

Inference

8. Why do you think Carmen is taking Luis to the school? *Accept any logical response about taking him to be punished; to the principal; to the authorities.*

9. How do you think Luis feels about himself? Why? *Accept any logical response supported with appropriate reasons.*

Evaluation

10. What would you do if you were Carmen and you saw someone writing on a wall? Explain your answer. *Accept any logical response supported with appropriate reasons.*

DIAGNOSIS

Diagnosis is the second part of the Preassessment section. Diagnosis is made up of the Elementary Spelling Inventory 1, the Names Test of Decoding, and the Interest Inventory.

Elementary Spelling Inventory I The Elementary Spelling Inventory I determines the stage of spelling instruction of your students. This test is administered to the whole class. You read the spelling list to the class, and students attempt to spell the words on a separate sheet of paper. Directions for administering the Elementary Spelling Inventory I begin on page 31 of this *Manual*. The Elementary Spelling Inventory I is located on page 33 of this *Manual*. The Student Diagnostic Chart, an Error Guide for the Elementary Spelling Inventory I, and a Feature Guide for the Elementary Spelling Inventory I are provided on pages 184–186 of this *Manual* and can be used to monitor student progress. For more information about the stages of spelling, see pages 164–165 of this *Manual*.

Names Test of Decoding The Names Test of Decoding by Patricia Cunningham diagnoses students' decoding skills. The test is administered on an individual basis. Students read the names on the list aloud to you, while you mark correct and incorrect pronunciations. Directions for administering The Names Test of Decoding begin on page 34 of this *Manual*. The Names Test of Decoding is located on page 35 of this *Manual*. The Student Diagnostic Chart is provided on page 184 of this *Manual* to monitor student progress.

Interest Inventory The Interest Inventory (optional) identifies your students' reading habits and attitudes. The Interest Inventory is located on page 36 of this *Manual*.

Administering the Elementary Spelling Inventory I

About the Elementary Spelling Inventory I

The Elementary Spelling Inventory I is designed to determine your students' stage of spelling instruction. You read a spelling list to the whole class, and students attempt to spell the words on a separate sheet of paper.

Directions

1. Before administering the Elementary Spelling Inventory I...

- Make one copy of the Elementary Spelling Inventory I Error Guide located on page 185 of this *Manual* for each student to grade each student's responses.

- Make one copy of the Elementary Spelling Inventory I Feature Guide located on page 186 of this *Manual* for each student to grade each student's responses.

- Make one copy of the Student Diagnostic Chart located on page 184 of this *Manual* for each student. Fill in the student information, and create an assessment folder for each student.

2. Administer the Elementary Spelling Inventory I.

Time: 20 minutes

- Instruct students to number 1–25 on a separate sheet of paper.

- Tell students that the Elementary Spelling Inventory I will give you valuable information about their ability to spell.

- Administer the the Elementary Spelling Inventory I following the instructions and possible script provided on page 33 of this *Manual*.

- After students complete the Inventory, ask them to put a star by the words that they think may not have been spelled correctly and to take a second try at these words. This provides an opportunity for reflection and gives you additional information about students' perception of their spelling skills.

3. Score the Elementary Spelling Inventory I.

This assessment may be scored now or at a later date after placement in Pearson materials has been determined.

- Score the papers, and give the ratio of correct answers to total responses, i.e., for 9 correct out of 25 responses, the ratio is 9/25. Score letter reversals as the intended letter and note for further diagnosis and observation. Do not be discouraged if students miss many words, as it is likely they will. However, their misspellings will provide valuable information as to their use of spelling strategies.

4. Interpret the results.

- Analyze student responses according to the Error Guide on page 185 of this *Manual* and the Feature Guide on page 186 of this *Manual* to interpret the types of errors students have made.

- Errors found in most students' spelling are probably listed in the Error Guide. For spellings not listed, write the incorrect spelling next to its closest match. After all responses are circled, look for:

  1. the orthographic, or correct spelling, features students know.

  2. what students use but confuse.

  3. the students' development level of spelling. Look for a cluster or pattern of errors, as boundaries may overlap. Students will not move clearly from one stage to the next.

- Review the Student Diagnostic Chart for recommendations about how to instruct students, based on the Elementary Spelling Inventory I results.

- Placement in the Within Word Pattern Developmental Stage or higher, reflects students' understanding of the alphabetic principle and basic phonics, indicating they do not need basic phonics instruction.

- Determine the focus of word study instruction. Use results to group students. Most spelling activities in *Caught Reading* are in the Syllables and Affixes stage. Additional activities are included in this *Manual*.

Elementary Spelling Inventory I

Instructions: Let the students know that you are administering this inventory to learn about how they spell. Let them know that this is not a test, but that they will be helping you be a better teacher by doing their best.

Sample script: "I am going to ask you to spell some words. Try to spell them the best you can. Some of the words will be easy to spell; some will be more difficult. When you do not know how to spell a word, spell it the best you can; write down all the sounds you hear."

Say the word once, read the sentence, and then say the word again. Work with groups of five words. You may want to stop testing when students miss three out of five words.

Have students check their papers for their names and the date.

Set One
1. bed — I hopped out of bed this morning. *bed*
2. ship — The ship sailed around the island. *ship*
3. when — When will you come back? *when*
4. lump — He had a lump on his head after he fell. *lump*
5. float — I can float on the water with my new raft. *float*

Set Two
6. train — I rode the train to the next town. *train*
7. place — I found a new place to put my books. *place*
8. drive — I learned to drive a car. *drive*
9. bright — The light is very bright. *bright*
10. shopping — Mother went shopping at the grocery store. *shopping*

Set Three
11. spoil — The food will spoil if it is not kept cool. *spoil*
12. serving — The restaurant is serving dinner tonight. *serving*
13. chewed — The dog chewed my favorite sweater yesterday. *chewed*
14. carries — She carries apples in her basket. *carries*
15. marched — We marched in the parade. *marched*

Set Four
16. shower — The shower in the bathroom was very hot. *shower*
17. cattle — The cowboy rounded up the cattle. *cattle*
18. favor — He did his brother a favor by taking out the trash. *favor*
19. ripen — The fruit will ripen over the next few days. *ripen*
20. cellar — I went down to the cellar for the can of paint. *cellar*

Set Five
21. pleasure — It was a pleasure to listen to the choir sing. *pleasure*
22. fortunate — It was fortunate that the driver had snow tires during the snowstorm. *fortunate*
23. confident — I am confident that we can win the game. *confident*
24. civilize — They had the idea that they could civilize the forest people. *civilize*
25. opposition — The coach said the opposition would give us a tough game. *opposition*

Administering The Names Test of Decoding

About The Names Test of Decoding

The Names Test of Decoding by Patricia Cunningham is designed to diagnose your students' decoding skills. You should administer the Names Test of Decoding to students who struggled with the Elementary Spelling Inventory I or the Level 3 and Level 4 Pretests.

Directions

1. Before administering The Names Test of Decoding…

- Make one copy of The Names Test of Decoding on page 35 of this *Manual* for each student and one copy for yourself. Students will read the names aloud to you from their copy. It might be helpful to laminate your copy so you do not have to keep replacing it.

2. Administer The Names Test of Decoding.

Time: 20 minutes

- Tell students that they will be reading a list of names aloud. Explain to them that it is like what you do when you take attendance.
- Ask individual students to read the names off the list.
- On the recording sheet, make a check above each name (first and last as separate entities) that is pronounced correctly. In the space above each name, write phonetic spellings for names that are mispronounced.

3. Score The Names Test of Decoding.

- Count a word correct if all syllables are pronounced correctly regardless of where the student places the accent.
- For words where the vowel pronunciation depends on which syllable the consonant is placed with, count them correct for either pronunciation. For example, either Ho/mer or Hom/er is acceptable.
- Count the number of names read correctly and analyze those mispronounced, looking for patterns of strength and weakness.
- Use the following abbreviations to classify the types of spelling errors:

  InCon: Initial Consonant; InConBl: Initial Consonant Blend; ConDgr: Consonant Digraph; ShVow: Short Vowel; LngVow: Long Vowel; VowDgr: Vowel Digraph; CtrVow: Center Vowel.

- Use the Student Diagnostic Chart on page 184 of this *Manual* to record the types of errors each student has made.

The Names Test of Decoding

by Patricia M. Cunningham
(with additional names by F.A. Dufflemeyer)

Jay Conway

Kimberly Blake

Cindy Sampson

Stanley Shaw

Flo Thornton

Ron Smitherman

Bernard Pendergraph

Austin Sheperd

Joan Brooks

Tim Cornell

Roberta Slade

Chester Wright

Wendy Swain

Dee Skidmore

Troy Whitlock

Shane Fletcher

Bertha Dale

Gene Loomis

Chuck Hoke

Homer Preston

Ginger Yale

Glen Spencer

Grace Brewster

Vance Middleton

Floyd Sheldon

Neal Wade

Thelma Rinehart

Yolanda Clark

Gus Quincy

Patrick Tweed

Fred Sherwood

Ned Westmoreland

Zane Anderson

Dean Bateman

Jake Murphy

Name _____ Date _____

INTEREST INVENTORY

Directions: Read each of the questions and circle the answer that best describes how you feel.

1. My family (mother, father, sister, brother, grandparent) read to me when I was little.
   not at all   a little   some   often

2. I like reading stories.
   not at all   a little   some   often

3. I like reading books I choose.
   not at all   a little   some   often

4. I like reading in my classes at school (history, language arts, science).
   not at all   a little   some   often

5. I like to read aloud.
   not at all   a little   some   often

6. I have trouble figuring out words.
   not at all   a little   some   often

7. Reading is boring.
   not at all   a little   some   often

8. I like to talk about things I read.
   not at all   a little   some   often

9. I am a fast reader.
   not at all   a little   some   often

10. I think I am a good reader.
    not at all   a little   some   often

Here is a list of reading materials that are usually read for pleasure. Circle any that you read on a regular basis:

magazines	fiction books (stories)	nonfiction books
short stories	poetry	newspapers
catalogs	computer text (Internet, games, etc.)	

ONGOING ASSESSMENT

Ongoing Assessment is designed to monitor your students' progress as they move through the *Caught Reading* program. Ongoing Assessment monitors fluency in the form of both reading rate and word recognition. This *Manual* provides Individual and Class Monitoring Charts for Ongoing Assessment. In this stage, students are encouraged to take part in scoring their results and updating the charts used to monitor progress. Ongoing Assessment includes:

Fluency Checks (Reading Rate) The Fluency Checks monitor your students' words per minute (WPM) reading rate and comprehension skills. The reading passages are located in the *Caught Reading* Worktexts. Directions for administering the Fluency Checks begin on page 38 of this *Manual*. The comprehension questions are located on pages 40–56 of this *Manual*. Students do timed reading and answer comprehension questions. The Fluency Checks can be administered as often as four times per Level. For more information about fluency, see pages 172–178 of this *Manual*.

Students should show consistent growth on the Fluency Checks. The ultimate goal is for students to reach reading rates at grade-level norms.

High Frequency Words Quizzes The High Frequency Words Quizzes monitor your students' word recognition skills. Many of these are words students will have encountered in the *Caught Reading* program. Directions for administering the High Frequency Words Quizzes begin on page 130 of this *Manual*. The High Frequency Words Quizzes are located on pages 131–137 of this *Manual*. You read words in context to students, and students spell the words on a separate sheet of paper. This requires students to recognize and comprehend in context the word they are being asked to spell. These quizzes can be administered seven times per Level.

Students should reach 100 percent mastery of the High Frequency Words Quizzes before moving to the next Level of *Caught Reading*.

Midway and Final Novel Comprehension Check The Midway and Final Novel Comprehension Checks monitor students' comprehension skills. The Midway and Final Novel Comprehension Checks are located in the *Teacher's Manual*. The comprehension questions test understanding of the Midway and Final Novels. Students answer comprehension questions after completing the Midway and Final Novels at a particular level. Individual Student Monthly Progress Monitoring Charts and a Monthly Class Summary Chart are provided on pages 187–189 of this *Manual* to monitor progress.

Students should score **80 percent or better** on the Comprehension Check. Students who do not score 80 percent may need to review the first half of the *Caught Reading* Level they are in.

Reteach Activities The Reteach Activities informally monitor decoding skills. The Reteach Activities are located in the *Caught Reading Teacher's Manual*. These informal assessment activities accompany the free lessons in the *Caught Reading* program.

Midway and Final Assessments The Midway and Final Assessments monitor both decoding skills and comprehension. The Midway and Final Assessments are located on pages 59–129 of this *Manual*. Students take the Midway Assessments when they have completed half of the *Caught Reading* Level that they are in. Individual Student Monthly Progress Monitoring Charts and a Monthly Class Summary Chart are provided on pages 187–189 of this *Manual* to monitor progress.

Students should score **80 percent or better** on these Assessments. Students who do not score 80 percent may need to review the material in the *Caught Reading* Worktext. Reteach suggestions are provided throughout the *Caught Reading Teacher's Manual*.

Administering the Fluency Checks

About the Fluency Checks

The Fluency Checks are designed to determine your students' words per minute (WPM) reading rate. The passages are found in the *Caught Reading* Worktexts.

For each Level of *Caught Reading*, there are as many as four Fluency Checks. Fluency Checks should ideally all contain the same number of words. However, because we selected the Fluency Checks from *Caught Reading* Worktexts, this is not possible. The upper Levels of the program have longer passages than the lower Levels. For this reason, the shorter passages have five questions, while the longer passages have 10 questions. The comprehension questions in this *Manual* ensure that students have not sacrificed comprehension for speed.

Fluency Checks can be administered as silent or oral reading. The process below describes a silent reading procedure. For oral reading, you may either use these same passages or any passage the student is currently studying. If you do not use the designated passage, have the student do a retelling to check comprehension.

Directions

1. Before administering the Fluency Checks...

- Obtain a copy of the *Caught Reading* Worktext that contains the passage for the Fluency Check being administered for each student.

- Determine which Fluency Check to administer to students. All Fluency Checks should be given BEFORE that passage has been studied as part of a lesson. Three per Level are provided (Level 7 has four). The last Fluency Check will serve as the Fluency Check Pretest for the Level that follows it.

- Make one copy of the appropriate Fluency Check on pages 40–56 of this *Manual* for each student. Students will record their answers on these sheets.

- Make one copy of the Fluency Check Student Recording Charts on pages 190–191 of this *Manual* for each student. Students record their scores on these charts. Students should create a fluency folder to keep their Fluency Check Student Recording Charts for future reference.

2. Administer the Fluency Checks.

Time: 20 minutes (per Fluency Check)

- Tell students that the Fluency Checks will help you determine how they are progressing through the *Caught Reading* program. Make sure students understand that they are not competing against the clock or their classmates.

- Distribute the Fluency Check for the appropriate passages, telling students to turn it face down on their desks.

- Tell students that they should have little difficulty reading the material. However, remind them that if they come to a word they do not know, they must keep going and complete the passage, figuring out the word the best way they can or skipping it for this reading. It is important that they work toward increasing their rate, yet still do their best to comprehend what they are reading.

- Tell students their reading will be timed even though the test will not be timed. Explain to students that you will be keeping track of the time on the board while they are reading the passage. Tell students that you will be marking the time on the board or overhead projector every 10 seconds (e.g., 10, 20, 30, 40, 50, 60, 70, etc.) until the last student has finished. Practice the process with students beforehand, making sure they know to look up at the numbers as soon as they finish and write down their time.

- Have students turn to the appropriate *Caught Reading* Worktext page for the Fluency Check, then to keep looking at you for the signal to start. They are not to look at the text.

- Check the clock for the starting time. When you are ready, tell students to begin reading.

- Tell students to look at the board and write down the last time on the board when they have finished reading.

- Tell students to answer the comprehension questions for the passage they read.

3. Score the Fluency Checks.

- Each student trades papers with a classmate, scoring while you read the correct answers to the class from the answer key on page 57–58 of this *Manual*.

- Students figure out their words per minute (WPM) rate. To figure the WPM, tell students to use the number of words divided by their time in the minutes. First, their time from the board, in seconds, must be divided by 60 to get their time in minutes. Then divide the number of words by their time in minutes (e.g. 210 ÷ 60 = 3.5; 325 ÷ 3.5 = 93 WPM). It is helpful to have students do this for themselves, but if that becomes too much of a math/time issue, you might want to do it for them or have one person do it quickly with a calculator.

- Record their WPM rate and score on Fluency Check on their Fluency Check Student Recording Charts, located on pages 190–191 of this *Manual*.

- Periodically conference with each student to verify correctness of data and rate.

Name _____   Date _____

LEVEL 1: Comprehension Questions   FLUENCY CHECK

Directions: Circle the correct answer for the questions that match the passage you are using. Follow your teacher's directions.

PRETEST: BEFORE LEVEL 1 INSTRUCTION:
PAGE 22: *FIRE* (162 WORDS)

1. My boss asked me why I hide my money at home, and I said,
   a. "It is safe at home."
   b. "I like to see my money."
   c. "I don't live near a bank."

2. Walking home from my job, I
   a. think about my money.
   b. hear sirens.
   c. see my house is on fire.

3. The next thing I do is
   a. go into the house.
   b. talk to the firemen.
   c. wait outside.

4. When I go into the house, the first thing I do is
   a. wake up Grandma.
   b. get the dog.
   c. find my mom.

5. We lost our house, but I am happy because
   a. I save my dog.
   b. my family is safe.
   c. we get a new house.

Number of Errors _____

FLUENCY CHECK #1: BEFORE LESSON 5
PAGE 24: *MY SISTER IS LOST* (156 WORDS)

1. My sister, Jen, is
   a. at school.
   b. at home.
   c. lost.

2. When my mother found out Jen was lost, she was
   a. angry.
   b. not happy.
   c. tired.

3. When I go out to find Jen, I
   a. take the bus.
   b. take the car.
   c. walk.

4. Jen's boss asked me if she was at
   a. the game.
   b. work.
   c. her friend's house.

5. When I go home, I say to my mom,
   a. "Call the police."
   b. "Go out and look for Jen."
   c. "Think about what to do!"

Number of Errors _____

Name _____   Date _____

LEVEL 1: Comprehension Questions   FLUENCY CHECK

Directions: Circle the correct answer for the questions that match the passage you are using. Follow your teacher's directions.

FLUENCY CHECK #2: BEFORE LESSON 10
PAGE 40:   *BIKE TEAM TRYOUTS*   (215 WORDS)

1. Kate and I are not friends, but she
   a. lives by me.
   b. knows my sister.
   c. is in a class with me.

2. The kids in class laugh at Kate because of
   a. the way she acts.
   b. the way she looks.
   c. what she says.

3. The coach of the bike team said that
   a. anyone who wants to can make the team.
   b. only 10 people can make the team.
   c. only boys can make the team.

4. While we are racing, Kate calls out to me to bike
   a. faster.
   b. in front of her.
   c. in back of her.

5. Kate helped me in the race because
   a. I helped her in class.
   b. she wanted me to like her.
   c. she is my neighbor.

Number of Errors _____

FLUENCY CHECK #3: BEFORE LESSON 16
(Also serves as Pretest for Level 2)
PAGES 59–60: *A NIGHT IN THE WOODS*
(294 WORDS)

1. Kate and Jen are going
   a. shopping together.
   b. to the movies.
   c. to cook and sleep in the woods.

2. Before they left, Kate's mom said,
   a. "Don't forget your jacket."
   b. "Don't forget the sleeping bags."
   c. "Don't forget the hot dogs."

3. The first thing Kate and Jen do when they go to the woods is
   a. unpack the hot dogs.
   b. build a fire.
   c. put out their sleeping bags.

4. When they discover they forgot the hot dogs, Jen can tell that Kate
   a. is not happy.
   b. wants to go back.
   c. wants to go to sleep.

5. When the girls see a light coming toward them, they
   a. hide in their sleeping bags.
   b. go back into the woods and wait.
   c. scream for help.

Number of Errors _____

Name _____ Date _____

LEVEL 2: Comprehension Questions   FLUENCY CHECK

Directions: Circle the correct answer for the questions that match the passage you are using. Follow your teacher's directions.

FLUENCY CHECK #1: BEFORE LESSON 6
PAGE 24: *THE BANK HOLD-UP* (195 WORDS)

1. I am at the bank waiting to see
   a. my friends.
   b. a movie.
   c. the bank teller.

2. The man behind me gives me a
   a. bad feeling.
   b. letter.
   c. good feeling.

3. He asks me to
   a. give him my money.
   b. help him with directions.
   c. save his place in line.

4. I try to get the bank teller to look because
   a. she knows the man.
   b. she can call for help.
   c. I am trying to smile at her.

5. When the cops get the man, he has
   a. $4,000.
   b. $50.
   c. no money.

Number of Errors _____

FLUENCY CHECK #2: BEFORE LESSON 11
PAGE 45: *THE VOTE* (291 WORDS)

1. I am trying to raise money for
   a. a homeless family.
   b. a school dance.
   c. the football team.

2. After some weeks, the school raises
   a. very little money.
   b. $400.
   c. $100.

3. Jared thinks the money should go to the baseball team to
   a. buy new uniforms.
   b. buy new equipment.
   c. get a coach.

4. Mu Lan wants to spend the money on the
   a. kids at school.
   b. band.
   c. homeless family.

5. When Jared and his friends asked the principal, she said
   a. the money should be shared with the band and baseball team.
   b. to save the money for a field trip.
   c. the students have to vote.

Number of Errors _____

Name _____ Date _____

LEVEL 2: Comprehension Questions   FLUENCY CHECK

Directions: Circle the correct answer for the questions that match the passage you are using. Follow your teacher's directions.

FLUENCY CHECK #3: BEFORE LESSON 14
(Also serves as Pretest for Level 3)
PAGES 55–56: *THE BIG WAVE* (417 WORDS)

1. As a big wave comes over the boat, dad screams,
   a. "Get the fish!"
   b. "Get your sister!"
   c. "Jump in the water!"

2. My dad tries to get help from a big ship by
   a. waving a big light.
   b. sending a signal.
   c. waving the paddle of the boat.

3. The people scream at us, but I
   a. can't see them.
   b. can't hear them.
   c. don't trust them.

4. The people try to throw us a line, but
   a. the line is not long enough.
   b. we can't get close enough to the other boat.
   c. my dad wants us to stay with the boat.

5. My dad wants to remember this day forever because we
   a. lost all the fish.
   b. could have won the championship.
   c. almost died.

Number of Errors _____

Name _____ Date _____

LEVEL 3: Comprehension Questions   FLUENCY CHECK

Directions: Circle the correct answer for the questions that match the passage you are using. Follow your teacher's directions.

FLUENCY CHECK #1: BEFORE LESSON 6
PAGE 24: *A PROBLEM FOR TOM* (314 WORDS)

1. The principal is looking everywhere for
   a. Tom.
   b. his stapler.
   c. a can of paint.

2. The principal is not happy because
   a. someone stayed home from school.
   b. someone wrote graffiti on the walls.
   c. someone stole a stapler from the class.

3. Tom didn't go to see the principal because
   a. he felt sick and wasn't at school.
   b. he wrote on the walls.
   c. he was too busy working.

4. Carmen goes with Tom because
   a. she wants to help.
   b. her class is on the way to the principal's office.
   c. she wrote on the school walls.

5. They both want to find out
   a. where their teacher was.
   b. who did the graffiti.
   c. the principal's name.

Number of Errors _____

FLUENCY CHECK #2: BEFORE LESSON 11
PAGES 40–41: *SATURDAY NIGHT* (439 WORDS)

1. Tom shows up on Saturday with his father's
   a. jacket.
   b. watch.
   c. truck.

2. Carmen decides to go with Tom to a shop because
   a. the truck broke down.
   b. she wants to buy a car.
   c. her dad works at the shop.

3. Tom checks the back of the truck because
   a. he left his tools there.
   b. Carmen heard something.
   c. he never looked back there before.

4. In the back of the truck, Tom finds a
   a. girl.
   b. hammer.
   c. blanket.

5. Inez came along because she
   a. likes the snow.
   b. likes trucks.
   c. wanted to see where they were going.

Number of Errors _____

Name _____   Date _____

LEVEL 3: Comprehension Questions   FLUENCY CHECK

Directions: Circle the correct answer for the questions that match the passage you are using. Follow your teacher's directions.

> **FLUENCY CHECK #3:** BEFORE LESSON 13
> (Also serves as Pretest for Level 4)
> PAGES 48–49: *LUIS AND THE BIG BIKE SALE*
> (435 WORDS)

1. Luis wants to buy a bike and
    a. save money.
    b. a puppy.
    c. a bike lock.

2. When Luis goes to the bike shop, there are
    a. no bikes left.
    b. many people in line.
    c. no sale prices on bikes.

3. Luis makes up a story to
    a. write for a school assignment.
    b. tell his mother.
    c. pass the time as he waits in line.

4. People think that there is a bike sale at
    a. Fire Mountain Bikes.
    b. Fire Lake Bicycles.
    c. Big Mountain Lake Bikes.

5. In the end, Luis
    a. stayed in line and bought a bike.
    b. went home for supper.
    c. went to a different bike store.

Number of Errors _____

Name _____ Date _____

LEVEL 4: Comprehension Questions   FLUENCY CHECK

Directions: Circle the correct answer for the questions that match the passage you are using. Follow your teacher's directions.

FLUENCY CHECK #1: BEFORE LESSON 4
PAGE 20: *A FISH STORY* (369 WORDS)

1. When Tom goes out fishing, the first thing he does is
   a. go to sleep.
   b. throw out his line.
   c. feel his line move.

2. Tom makes the fish work by
   a. moving the line up and down.
   b. making the boat go fast.
   c. letting the line out and then pulling it in.

3. Tom has a problem because
   a. the fish is bigger than he is.
   b. the fish is angry.
   c. the boat is too small to hold the fish.

4. Tom is scared because
   a. he is alone.
   b. the shark is moving faster than the boat.
   c. the shark is eating his fish.

5. When Tom gets back and tells everyone what happened, they
   a. treat him like a hero.
   b. ask if they can see his fish.
   c. don't believe his story about catching a big fish.

Number of Errors _____

FLUENCY CHECK #2: BEFORE LESSON 10
PAGE 43: *JARED'S CAR* (305 WORDS)

1. Jared is frustrated about his car because
   a. he doesn't know how to fix it.
   b. something is always going wrong.
   c. the repair shop is closed.

2. Jared believes that things made in the old days are better because they were
   a. cheaper.
   b. easier to get.
   c. made from rock.

3. Jared gave Tyrone a look because he
   a. is not sure whether to believe him.
   b. thinks he is smart.
   c. talks too much.

4. Tyrone tells Jared that the glass windows on his car are made from
   a. metal.
   b. water and air.
   c. ground up rock from the beach.

5. When it comes down to it, Tyrone says that Jared's car is made of
   a. metal.
   b. rock.
   c. ground up rock from the beach.

Number of Errors _____

Name _____ Date _____

LEVEL 4: Comprehension Questions   FLUENCY CHECK

Directions: Circle the correct answer for the questions that match the passage you are using. Follow your teacher's directions.

FLUENCY CHECK #3: BEFORE LESSON 15
(Also serves as Pretest for Level 5)
PAGES 64–65: *COMPUTERS AND ROBOTS*
(438 WORDS)

1. Machines help us live better, but they
   a. cost us money.
   b. change our lives.
   c. make our lives more complicated.

2. The computer is a machine that
   a. lets us talk with people on other planets.
   b. makes us work harder.
   c. helps us think.

3. Robots are machines that
   a. look like humans.
   b. work together with computers.
   c. run on batteries.

4. A well-known scientist
   a. was sick and helpless.
   b. was the first man to make a robot.
   c. used a robot to talk for him.

5. Someday, the Earth may belong to robots and computers, but they will not
   a. fix cars.
   b. do housework.
   c. teach students.

Number of Errors _____

Name _____   Date _____

LEVEL 5: Comprehension Questions   FLUENCY CHECK

Directions: Circle the correct answer for the questions that match the passage you are using. Follow your teacher's directions.

FLUENCY CHECK #1: BEFORE LESSON 2
PAGES 13–14: *FANNIE LOU HAMER IN POLITICS*
(349 WORDS)

1. Hamer talked to African Americans everywhere and told them
    a. to work very hard.
    b. that she was running for president.
    c. that they had the right to vote.

2. Fannie Lou Hamer was from
    a. California.
    b. Mississippi.
    c. Texas.

3. In 1963, Fannie took the voting test again and
    a. failed because she wasn't ready.
    b. passed the voting test.
    c. didn't finish taking the test.

4. Fannie wasn't able to vote because
    a. she didn't have the money to vote.
    b. she didn't believe in voting.
    c. she was busy at work.

5. The law that was passed saying that no one could be stopped from voting was the
    a. Fannie Lou Hamer Act.
    b. Mississippi Act of 1960.
    c. Voting Rights Act.

Number of Errors _____

FLUENCY CHECK #2: BEFORE LESSON 5
PAGES 25–26: *THE HISTORY OF JEANS*
(228 WORDS)

1. In 1850, Levi Strauss went to find riches in
    a. California.
    b. Sacramento.
    c. Alabama.

2. To make tents and covered wagons, miners bought
    a. cow hides.
    b. Levi Strauss's strong cloth.
    c. alligator skin.

3. Levi Strauss used his strong cloth to make
    a. pants.
    b. jackets.
    c. sweaters.

4. Strauss made them even stronger by
    a. gluing them.
    b. doubling up the cloth.
    c. adding metal rivets.

5. Strauss's cloth is still used to make
    a. wagon covers.
    b. jeans.
    c. tents.

Number of Errors _____

Name _____   Date _____

LEVEL 5: Comprehension Questions   FLUENCY CHECK

Directions: Circle the correct answer for the questions that match the passage you are using. Follow your teacher's directions.

FLUENCY CHECK #3: BEFORE LESSON 11 (Also serves as Pretest for Level 6):
PAGES 51–52: *CÉSAR CHÁVEZ: CHAMPION OF THE FARMWORKERS* (566 WORDS)

1. When he was 15, César Chávez stopped going to school because he
   a. wasn't learning anything.
   b. had to help his family make a living.
   c. was moving to a new house.

2. Chávez made his living by
   a. repairing cars.
   b. flying an airplane.
   c. working in the fields.

3. Farmworkers had a lot of problems because
   a. they made too little money.
   b. there weren't enough workers.
   c. they didn't want to work hard.

4. In 1962, Chávez started a
   a. protest march.
   b. club for grape growers.
   c. farmworkers union.

5. Chávez believed that the workers
   a. should be religious.
   b. had a right to a fair living.
   c. should use violence if necessary.

6. In 1965, Chávez's union went on strike against the
   a. cotton growers.
   b. grape growers.
   c. orange growers.

7. The grape growers held out because they didn't want to
   a. lose money.
   b. change how they ran their grape fields.
   c. hire the farm workers.

8. Chávez did not believe in
   a. violence.
   b. the Bible.
   c. working hard.

9. To stop the violence, Chávez
   a. called the police.
   b. stopped the strike.
   c. fasted.

10. By the late 1960s, the growers had
    a. lost millions of dollars.
    b. almost 200 farms.
    c. stopped hiring farmworkers.

Number of Errors _____

Name _____ Date _____

LEVEL 6: Comprehension Questions   FLUENCY CHECK

Directions: Circle the correct answer for the questions that match the passage you are using. Follow your teacher's directions.

FLUENCY CHECK #1: BEFORE LESSON 4
PAGES 22–23: *THE OLD GREEN BUILDING, PART 2* (419 WORDS)

1. César says good night to his mother as
   a. he goes to bed.
   b. he goes out with Mike.
   c. his mother goes to bed.

2. Down the street, Mike showed César
   a. a long red car.
   b. a new blue bicycle.
   c. his new clothes.

3. Mike told César to "lighten up" because they
   a. would soon be rich.
   b. were going to do some good.
   c. were going to eat dinner.

4. César was quiet because he
   a. trusted Mike.
   b. was afraid of Mike.
   c. didn't know how to stop Mike.

5. After they parked, César and Mike
   a. waited until the cars went by.
   b. hid on the floor of the car.
   c. counted the cars going by.

6. When they saw the words, "Keep Out,"
   a. Mike got angry.
   b. César didn't want to go in.
   c. they knew it might be dangerous.

7. The boys could not get in the building from the
   a. front.
   b. side.
   c. street.

8. Behind the building, they found
   a. a large trash bin.
   b. an abandoned car.
   c. a big lot with 20 or 30 cars.

9. They were able to get into the building through
   a. an unlocked window.
   b. a crack in the wall.
   c. a hole in the roof.

10. Inside the building, it was dark because
    a. they forgot their flashlight.
    b. the windows were covered with boards.
    c. all the lights had been broken.

Number of Errors _____

Name _____   Date _____

LEVEL 6: Comprehension Questions   FLUENCY CHECK

Directions: Circle the correct answer for the questions that match the passage you are using. Follow your teacher's directions.

FLUENCY CHECK #32: BEFORE LESSON 6
PAGES 32–33: *THE OLD GREEN BUILDING, PART 4* (498 WORDS)

1. César tells Mike that he wants to go to
    a. get help.
    b. get something to eat.
    c. check on Mike's car.

2. Mike told César that
    a. he didn't like spiders.
    b. he was afraid of spiders.
    c. he should not worry about the spider.

3. Mike was afraid of
    a. large spiders.
    b. killer spiders.
    c. any spiders.

4. César tried to get to Mike through a
    a. locked door.
    b. broken window.
    c. hole in the wall.

5. To get through the spider webs, César
    a. ran really fast.
    b. used a broom to get them down.
    c. put a paper bag over his head.

6. César found Mike by
    a. feeling his way toward the sound of Mike's voice.
    b. crawling along the floor.
    c. using a stick to poke along in front of him.

7. The spider webs were
    a. very sticky.
    b. full of poison spiders.
    c. too thick to see through.

8. César helped Mike by
    a. carrying him out of the building.
    b. giving him a paper bag and leading him out.
    c. calling for help.

9. What they got outside, Mike didn't want to
    a. go back home.
    b. go back for the money.
    c. tell anyone what happened.

10. César knew that Mike
    a. had learned a lesson.
    b. would go back into the building.
    c. could not read the sign on the door.

Number of Errors _____

Name _____   Date _____

LEVEL 6: Comprehension Questions   FLUENCY CHECK

Directions: Circle the correct answer for the questions that match the passage you are using. Follow your teacher's directions.

FLUENCY CHECK #3: BEFORE LESSON 10 (Also serves as Pretest for Level 7)
PAGES 54–56: *MATTHEW HENSON, EXPLORER, PART 2* (980 WORDS)

1. Between 1891 and 1897, Henson and Peary made three trips to
   a. Alaska.
   b. Greenland.
   c. America.

2. People who live in the south of Greenland are called
   a. Indians.
   b. Inuits.
   c. Greenlanders.

3. The Inuits showed Henson how to
   a. live in the snow.
   b. make sleds and drive dog teams.
   c. find his way back home.

4. On the second trip, most of the people were
   a. Inuits.
   b. Eskimos.
   c. scientists.

5. Early on, there was trouble because
   a. a wave hit their house.
   b. the dogs died.
   c. the men couldn't get along.

6. No one wanted to follow Peary and his men north because
   a. there were no animals and nothing to eat.
   b. there was a large creature there, and they were afraid.
   c. they did not like Peary and his men.

7. On one of the trips,
   a. it snowed for weeks.
   b. they found one of their men frozen.
   c. Henson and Peary gave up.

8. Close to the water, Peary saw and killed a
   a. wild boar.
   b. polar bear.
   c. musk ox.

9. A musk ox was going to kill
   a. Henson.
   b. the dogs.
   c. Peary.

10. There was only one dog left when Henson and Peary returned to their base because
    a. the others ran away.
    b. they started with one dog.
    c. they were forced to eat the other dogs to survive.

Number of Errors _____

Name _____   Date _____

LEVEL 7: Comprehension Questions   FLUENCY CHECK

Directions: Circle the correct answer for the questions that match the passage you are using. Follow your teacher's directions.

FLUENCY CHECK #1: BEFORE LESSON 4
PAGES 21–23: *NEW IN THE CITY* (709 WORDS)

1. The summer before, Dan had a job
   a. cleaning houses.
   b. fixing cars.
   c. cooking in a fast-food place.

2. Dan was offered a job at Henson Homes by
   a. his father.
   b. his uncle.
   c. a family friend.

3. When Dan got the job, he
   a. felt happy.
   b. had to move to the city.
   c. had to buy a car.

4. The job skills Dan would learn were
   a. fixing computers.
   b. building homes.
   c. making out bills and keeping the books.

5. Dan went to the corner to buy
   a. a newspaper to look for an apartment.
   b. tomatoes for dinner.
   c. a comic book to read.

6. On the way to the corner, Dan met
   a. a bum on the street.
   b. an old friend.
   c. a young woman.

7. The girl needed change to buy a
   a. bus ticket.
   b. newspaper.
   c. soda pop.

8. The part of the paper Dan wanted to read was the
   a. want ads.
   b. movie section.
   c. local news.

9. Dan wanted to talk to the woman, but
   a. he was in a hurry to get home.
   b. she did not seem interested in making new friends.
   c. she was talking to someone else.

10. The newspaper ad said,
    a. "3 rooms for $250.00."
    b. "No pets allowed."
    c. "Call Matt."

Number of Errors _____

Name _____   Date _____

LEVEL 7: Comprehension Questions   FLUENCY CHECK

Directions: Circle the correct answer for the questions that match the passage you are using. Follow your teacher's directions.

FLUENCY CHECK #2: BEFORE LESSON 8
PAGES 40–41: *A GREAT APARTMENT* (793 WORDS)

1. The apartment Dan was looking for was called
   a. The Green Building.
   b. The Woods.
   c. The Green Space.

2. On the telephone, the man had said that
   a. many people are interested in the apartment.
   b. no loud music is allowed.
   c. you better come quick.

3. The newspaper ad said that the apartment had
   a. five rooms.
   b. an all-electric kitchen.
   c. a pool and jacuzzi.

4. When Dan was shown the apartment, it was
   a. better than he ever imagined.
   b. a very quiet and large place.
   c. not like the ad described.

5. On the back of the form in small words, it says he
   a. must stay in the apartment for one year.
   b. must stay in the apartment for two years.
   c. can move out if he doesn't like it.

6. Dan is angry and tells the man
   a. his rent is unfair.
   b. his ad is not true.
   c. he's not interested.

7. As he is leaving, he sees a sign saying
   a. room for rent.
   b. two-bedroom apartment for rent.
   c. roommate wanted.

8. Dan can move into the room if he can
   a. pass a test.
   b. prove he has a job.
   c. pay an extra $500.

9. As Dan stands alone in his new apartment, he looks out at
   a. his uncle.
   b. his dream car.
   c. the young woman from before.

10. Dan opens the window to call out to her, but
    a. he doesn't know her name.
    b. she is too far down the street.
    c. he had lost his voice.

Number of Errors _____

Name _____   Date _____

LEVEL 7: Comprehension Questions   FLUENCY CHECK

Directions: Circle the correct answer for the questions that match the passage you are using. Follow your teacher's directions.

FLUENCY CHECK #3: BEFORE LESSON 10 (Also serves as Final Check for *Caught Reading*)
PAGES 51–52: *A GOOD USED CAR* (712 WORDS)

1. Dan wanted to buy a
   a. good used car.
   b. brand new radio.
   c. sofa for his apartment.

2. On the radio, Dan hears an ad for
   a. the "Good Guys."
   b. used cars at cheap prices.
   c. the "Car Guys."

3. The ad says that if you don't have enough money,
   a. don't try to buy a car.
   b. put $100 down and take it home tonight.
   c. we'll loan you the money.

4. Dan goes over to the car lot
   a. on the bus.
   b. in a taxi.
   c. on his bike.

5. Fast Jake wants to take Dan and the woman
   a. out to dinner.
   b. into his office.
   c. out for a test drive.

6. Dan can't buy the weekly special car because it
   a. is too expensive.
   b. is not for sale.
   c. has already been sold.

7. The woman knows a lot about cars because she
   a. owns several.
   b. has been around cars all of her life.
   c. has read a lot of books about cars.

8. The young woman's name is
   a. Mary.
   b. Lisa.
   c. Dana.

9. The young woman looks at the engine and says,
   a. "It looks great!"
   b. "It needs a ring job!"
   c. "It must be a fast car!"

10. She tells Dan that she could help him
    a. buy a car.
    b. buy new clothes.
    c. learn to drive.

Number of Errors _____

Name _____ Date _____

LEVEL 7: Comprehension Questions FLUENCY CHECK

Directions: Circle the correct answer for the questions that match the passage you are using. Follow your teacher's directions.

FLUENCY CHECK #4: BEFORE LESSON 12
PAGES 60–62: *DANA GETS A JOB* (824 WORDS)

1. Dana went to see Mr. Henson to
   a. interview for a job.
   b. pay back money.
   c. take him to lunch.

2. Mr. Henson is looking for someone with
   a. good looks.
   b. experience.
   c. a good attitude.

3. Dana is good with
   a. numbers.
   b. computers.
   c. running machines.

4. Mr. Henson's business owns a lot of
   a. trucks and power tools.
   b. stock.
   c. property.

5. Dana heard about the job from
   a. a newspaper advertisement.
   b. an old friend.
   c. her father.

6. Mr. Henson goes to the corner of the room to talk with
   a. Dana's mother.
   b. Dan.
   c. Dan's uncle.

7. Mr. Henson hires her because
   a. she helped Dan not buy a car.
   b. she is very experienced at computers.
   c. he knows her mother.

8. Dana didn't think Dan needed her help because
   a. he was driving a new car.
   b. another girl was helping him.
   c. he never called her.

9. Dan invites Dana to dinner because he
   a. needs her help in looking at a car.
   b. owes her money.
   c. feels bad she didn't get the job.

10. As she leaves, Dana feels that
    a. her life is really taking off at last.
    b. she made a mistake by taking the job.
    c. Dan really doesn't like her.

Number of Errors _____

Fluency Check Answer Keys

LEVEL 1 ANSWER KEY

PRETEST: BEFORE LEVEL 1 INSTRUCTION:
PAGE 22: *FIRE* (162 WORDS)

1. b **2.** c **3.** a **4.** c **5.** b

FLUENCY CHECK #1: BEFORE LESSON 5
PAGE 24: *MY SISTER IS LOST* (156 WORDS)

1. c **2.** b **3.** b **4.** a **5.** c

FLUENCY CHECK #2: BEFORE LESSON 10
PAGE 40: *BIKE TEAM TRYOUTS* (213 WORDS)

1. c **2.** c **3.** b **4.** c **5.** a

FLUENCY CHECK #3: BEFORE LESSON 16
(Also serves as Pretest for Level 2)
PAGES 59–60: *A NIGHT IN THE WOODS* (295 WORDS)

1. c **2.** b **3.** c **4.** a **5.** b

WORDS PER MINUTE READING NORMS

GRADE	1	2	3	4	5	6	7	8
WPM	<81	82–108	109–130	131–147	148–161	162–174	175–185	186–197

LEVEL 2 ANSWER KEY

PRETEST:
USE THE SCORE FROM FLUENCY CHECK #3 IN LESSON 1.
NOTE: If the student is entering the program at this level, use Fluency Check #3 from Level 1 as the Pretest.

FLUENCY CHECK #1: BEFORE LESSON 6
PAGE 24: *THE BANK HOLD-UP* (194 WORDS)

1. c **2.** a **3.** a **4.** b **5.** a

FLUENCY CHECK #2: BEFORE LESSON 11
PAGE 45: *THE VOTE* (291 WORDS)

1. a **2.** b **3.** c **4.** b **5.** c

FLUENCY CHECK #3: BEFORE LESSON 14
(Also serves as Pretest for Level 3)
PAGES 55–56: *THE BIG WAVE* (417 WORDS)

1. b **2.** a **3.** b **4.** b **5.** c

WORDS PER MINUTE READING NORMS

GRADE	1	2	3	4	5	6	7	8
WPM	<81	82–108	109–130	131–147	148–161	162–174	175–185	186–197

LEVEL 3 ANSWER KEY

PRETEST
USE THE SCORE FROM FLUENCY CHECK #3 IN LEVEL 2.
NOTE: If the student is entering the program at this level, use Fluency Check #3 from Level 2 as the Pretest.

FLUENCY CHECK #1: BEFORE LESSON 6
PAGE 24: *A PROBLEM FOR TOM* (315 WORDS)

1. a **2.** b **3.** a **4.** a **5.** b

FLUENCY CHECK #2: BEFORE LESSON 11
PAGES 40–41: *SATURDAY NIGHT* (320 WORDS)

1. c **2.** a **3.** b **4.** a **5.** c

FLUENCY CHECK #3: BEFORE LESSON 13
(Also serves as Pretest for Level 4)
PAGES 48–49: *LUIS AND THE BIG BIKE SALE* (337 WORDS)

1. a **2.** b **3.** c **4.** a **5.** a

WORDS PER MINUTE READING NORMS

GRADE	1	2	3	4	5	6	7	8
WPM	<81	82–108	109–130	131–147	148–161	162–174	175–185	186–197

LEVEL 4 ANSWER KEY

PRETEST:
USE THE SCORE FROM FLUENCY CHECK #3 IN LEVEL 3.
NOTE: If the student is entering the program at this level, use Fluency Check #3 from Level 3 as the Pretest.

FLUENCY CHECK #1: BEFORE LESSON 4
PAGE 20: *A FISH STORY* (371 WORDS)

1. b **2.** c **3.** a **4.** b **5.** c

FLUENCY CHECK #2: BEFORE LESSON 10
PAGE 43: *JARED'S CAR* (305 WORDS)

1. b **2.** c **3.** a **4.** c **5.** b

FLUENCY CHECK #3: BEFORE LESSON 15
(Also serves as Pretest for Level 5)
PAGES 64–65: *COMPUTERS AND ROBOTS* (305 WORDS)

1. b **2.** c **3.** b **4.** c **5.** b

WORDS PER MINUTE READING NORMS

GRADE	1	2	3	4	5	6	7	8
WPM	<81	82–108	109–130	131–147	148–161	162–174	175–185	186–197

Fluency Check Answer Keys (Continued)

LEVEL 5 ANSWER KEY

PRETEST:
USE THE SCORE FROM FLUENCY CHECK #3 IN LEVEL 4.
NOTE: If the student is entering the program at this level, use Fluency Check #3 from Level 4 as the Pretest.

FLUENCY CHECK #1: BEFORE LESSON 2
PAGES 13–14: *FANNIE LOU HAMER IN POLITICS*
(350 WORDS)

1. c   **2.** b   **3.** b   **4.** a   **5.** c

FLUENCY CHECK #2: BEFORE LESSON 5
PAGES 25–26: *THE HISTORY OF JEANS* (230 WORDS)

1. a   **2.** b   **3.** a   **4.** c   **5.** b

FLUENCY CHECK #3: BEFORE LESSON 11
(Also serves as Pretest for Level 6):
PAGES 51–52: *CÉSAR CHÁVEZ: CHAMPION OF THE FARMWORKERS* (550 WORDS)

1. b   **2.** c   **3.** a   **4.** c   **5.** b
6. b   **7.** b   **8.** a   **9.** c   **10.** a

WORDS PER MINUTE READING NORMS

GRADE	1	2	3	4	5	6	7	8
WPM	<81	82–108	109–130	131–147	148–161	162–174	175–185	186–197

LEVEL 6 ANSWER KEY

PRETEST:
USE THE SCORE FROM FLUENCY CHECK #3 IN LEVEL 5.
NOTE: If the student is entering the program at this level, use Fluency Check #3 from Level 5 as the Pretest.

FLUENCY CHECK #1: BEFORE LESSON 4
PAGES 22–23: *THE OLD GREEN BUILDING, PART 2*
(414 WORDS)

1. b   **2.** a   **3.** b   **4.** c   **5.** a
6. b   **7.** a   **8.** c   **9.** a   **10.** b

FLUENCY CHECK #2: BEFORE LESSON 6
PAGES 32–33: *THE OLD GREEN BUILDING, PART 4*
(438 WORDS)

1. a   **2.** b   **3.** c   **4.** a   **5.** c
6. a   **7.** c   **8.** b   **9.** b   **10.** a

FLUENCY CHECK #3: BEFORE LESSON 10
(Also serves as Pretest for Level 7)
PAGES 54–55: *MATTHEW HENSON, EXPLORER, PART 2*
(681 WORDS)

1. b   **2.** b   **3.** b   **4.** c   **5.** a
6. a   **7.** b   **8.** c   **9.** c   **10.** c

WORDS PER MINUTE READING NORMS

GRADE	1	2	3	4	5	6	7	8
WPM	<81	82–108	109–130	131–147	148–161	162–174	175–185	186–197

LEVEL 7 ANSWER KEY

PRETEST:
USE THE SCORE FROM FLUENCY CHECK #3 IN LEVEL 6.
NOTE: If the student is entering the program at this level, use Fluency Check #3 from Level 6 as the Pretest.

FLUENCY CHECK #1: BEFORE LESSON 4
PAGES 21–23: *NEW IN THE CITY* (645 WORDS)

1. c   **2.** b   **3.** b   **4.** c   **5.** a
6. c   **7.** b   **8.** a   **9.** b   **10.** a

FLUENCY CHECK #2: BEFORE LESSON 8
PAGES 40–41: *A GREAT APARTMENT* (814 WORDS)

1. b   **2.** a   **3.** b   **4.** c   **5.** a
6. c   **7.** a   **8.** b   **9.** c   **10.** a

FLUENCY CHECK #3: BEFORE LESSON 10
(Also serves as Final Check for *Caught Reading*)
PAGES 51–52: *A GOOD USED CAR* (720 WORDS)

1. a   **2.** c   **3.** b   **4.** a   **5.** c
6. c   **7.** b   **8.** c   **9.** b   **10.** a

This check can be used as a Posttest for the *Caught Reading* series or as an extra fluency check.

FLUENCY CHECK #4: BEFORE LESSON 12
PAGES 60–62: *DANA GETS A JOB* (780 WORDS)

1. a   **2.** b   **3.** c   **4.** a   **5.** a
6. c   **7.** a   **8.** c   **9.** a   **10.** a

WORDS PER MINUTE READING NORMS

GRADE	1	2	3	4	5	6	7	8
WPM	<81	82–108	109–130	131–147	148–161	162–174	175–185	186–197

Name: _____ Date: _____

FINAL ASSESSMENT—*GETTING READY*

A. Unscramble the Words

Below is a series of words to unscramble. When you unscramble the word, write it.
Then read the word and place a check mark next to the word, indicating that you read it.

	Example			Write it.	Read it.
	t	a	th	that	✓
1.	ch	p	o	_____	❑
2.	i	ck	k	_____	❑
3.	d	b	a	_____	❑
4.	n	p	e	_____	❑
5.	f	ll	i	_____	❑
6.	a	p	ss	_____	❑
7.	u	ff	c	_____	❑
8.	ea	m	t	_____	❑
9.	n	oi	c	_____	❑
10.	ee	wh	l	_____	❑
11.	b	t	oa	_____	❑
12.	ar	m	f	_____	❑
13.	l	ue	b	_____	❑
14.	r	t	ue	_____	❑
15.	n	au	t	_____	❑
16.	g	ew	r	_____	❑
17.	th	ee	r	_____	❑
18.	n	d	e	_____	❑
19.	ay	l	p	_____	❑
20.	ee	r	t	_____	❑

Name: _____   Date: _____

B. Substitute Sounds and Letters

Look at each word and fill in the blank to make a word. If you can think of words to make using other letters, write these words, too.

Example: c __ p   _cap, cop, cup_

1. p __ n   _____
2. m a __   _____
3. __ u t   _____
4. f __ n   _____
5. t a __   _____

6. __ u g   _____
7. h __ t   _____
8. t __ p   _____
9. __ i d   _____
10. p a __   _____

C. Delete Sounds and Letters

Look at each word. Delete one letter to make a new word.

Example: plan   _pan_
              plane   _plan_

1. play   _____
2. hide   _____
3. cube   _____
4. free   _____
5. blank   _____

6. clap   _____
7. frog   _____
8. mate   _____
9. coat   _____
10. aunt   _____

D. Sort the Words

Read each word in the Word Bank. Sort and write each word under the correct category.

WORD BANK			
peach	cute	write	chip
mate	catch	sled	wheel
drove	mud	frog	send

Short-vowel words   **Long-vowel words**

_____   _____

_____   _____

_____   _____

_____   _____

_____   _____

_____

60

Name: _____ Date: _____

E. Fill in the Blanks

Read each sentence and fill in the correct word. The words can be found in the Word Bank. Use each word once.

WORD BANK		
climb	brown	swimming
saddle	streets	hike
trail	stream	tripped

1. When you _____, follow the _____.
2. Be careful when you _____.
3. I see a _____ bear in the woods.
4. Pam likes to go _____ in the pond.
5. Jeff _____ over a large log.
6. I will put a _____ on the horse.
7. The puppy drank from the _____.
8. The _____ are wet from the rain.

F. Make a Bigger Word

Look at the words in each box. Combine a word in one box with a word in the other box to make a bigger word. Write each compound word below.

soft	port
snow	light
rain	bow
to	flake
sun	day
air	ball

1. _____ 4. _____
2. _____ 5. _____
3. _____ 6. _____

G. Is It a Prefix or Suffix?

Read each sentence. Underline the words that contain a prefix. Circle the words that contain a suffix. Remember, a prefix is a word part, or chunk, found at the beginning of a word. A suffix is a word part, or chunk, found at the end of a word.

1. Please do not unfasten your seat belt.
2. I would like to refill my drink.
3. José is hopeful that it will be a sunny day.
4. We are careful when we ski down the slope.
5. My shirt is washable.
6. Sam and Sally dislike snakes.

Name: _____ Date: _____

GETTING READY ASSESSMENT CHECKLIST

Place letter cards on the table. Say each word slowly. Have students take turns saying and spelling each word. Record student performance here for your records.

Student name	Nonsense or real word	Score	Notes
1. _____	_____	_____	_____
2. _____	_____	_____	_____
3. _____	_____	_____	_____
4. _____	_____	_____	_____
5. _____	_____	_____	_____
6. _____	_____	_____	_____
7. _____	_____	_____	_____
8. _____	_____	_____	_____
9. _____	_____	_____	_____
10. _____	_____	_____	_____
11. _____	_____	_____	_____
12. _____	_____	_____	_____
13. _____	_____	_____	_____
14. _____	_____	_____	_____
15. _____	_____	_____	_____
16. _____	_____	_____	_____
17. _____	_____	_____	_____
18. _____	_____	_____	_____
19. _____	_____	_____	_____
20. _____	_____	_____	_____
21. _____	_____	_____	_____
22. _____	_____	_____	_____
23. _____	_____	_____	_____
24. _____	_____	_____	_____
25. _____	_____	_____	_____
26. _____	_____	_____	_____
27. _____	_____	_____	_____
28. _____	_____	_____	_____
29. _____	_____	_____	_____
30. _____	_____	_____	_____

Score: _____

Name: _____ Date: _____

MIDWAY ASSESSMENT LEVEL 1

A. Use the words in the box to fill in the blanks. Use each word one time.

am	friend	game	happy	house
little	make	people	players	problem
sick	sister	thinking	waiting	with

Jen wants to go to the big game. The _____ is on Saturday. The coach and the players are _____ for Saturday. So is Jen.

"I wanted to go _____ you," says Jen's little sister, "but I can't. I _____ sick."

"That is a _____," Jen says to her _____. "I am sorry that you are _____, but you cannot go with me. You can _____ people at the game sick, and then the problem is bigger." Jen does not have a happy sister.

On Saturday, Jen calls her friend Tom. "My _____ sister is not happy," Jen says to Tom. "She cannot go to the game. She is sick," says Jen. "Can we make my little sister _____?"

Tom thinks that he can find a way to make Jen's little sister happy. He tells Jen what he is _____ about. Then he walks to Jen's house to get Jen. Jen and Tom walk to the game.

The players make a lot of hits, and the big game makes a lot of _____ happy. Tom goes to talk to the players. Then he comes back to talk to Jen. "The players want to do it," says Tom. "The players will come by the _____ to see your little sister. She can't come out of the house, but the players can talk to her in the house."

Jen's little sister sees the _____. They are in a big truck. They talk to Jen's little sister, who is in the house. The players talk with Jen's little sister and make her happy.

"Tom," says Jen, "you make little problems out of big problems. You are a _____—a BIG friend!"

"I'm happy that you are my big sister," says Jen's little sister.

"And I am happy that you are my little sister," says Jen.

Name: _____   Date: _____

B. Circle the words that end the same way as the first word. Then choose a word you circled to fill in the blank.

| make | 1. | Jake | fake | ran | cake |

Jen makes a _____.

| ad | 2. | play | dad | had | mad |

My _____ has the biggest truck.

| ran | 3. | add | an | Dan | can |

My friend is _____.

| all | 4. | tall | hall | has | call |

My mom is big and _____.

| say | 5. | day | plan | play | Jen |

I go to school the next _____.

| walk | 6. | talk | chalk | wall | make |

I like to _____ to that girl.

| not | 7. | top | hot | stop | got |

A _____ car is a big problem.

C. How many words can you name that end like *say*, *all*, *walk*, *not*, and *make*? Write them on the lines.

say	all	walk	not	make
_____	_____	_____	_____	_____
_____	_____	_____	_____	_____
_____	_____	_____	_____	_____
_____	_____	_____	_____	_____
_____	_____	_____	_____	_____
_____	_____	_____	_____	_____

Name: _____ Date: _____

D. Read each base word. Add an ending *s*, *ed*, *ing*, *er*, or *'s* to make a new word. If the ending does not make a new word, leave the line blank.

Base Word	s	ed	ing	er	's
1. dog					
2. big					
3. talk					
4. hall					
5. hit					
6. Dan					
7. kid					
8. stop					
9. find					
10. truck					

E. Read each sentence. Choose the best word to complete the sentence.

1. We _____ to the school.   **walks   walking   walked**

2. We went by _____ house.   **Jen   Jen's   Jens**

3. I _____ need friends like Dan.   **don't   can't   I'm**

4. Do you have car _____?   **problem   problems   problem's**

5. My _____ car has a problem.   **friend's   friends   friend**

6. I'm _____ to make a lot of money.   **goes   go   going**

7. That is Jake's CD _____.   **plays   player   play**

8. Jake talks a lot. He is a _____.   **talking   talk   talker**

Name: _____ Date: _____

FINAL ASSESSMENT LEVEL 1

A. Use the words in the box to fill in the blanks. Use each word one time.

players	talk	sister	lost	school
happy	does	problem	about	hit
teamwork	game	college	man	bus

"Get going," Coach says. "Get on the bus."

The team walks to the bus. We are not talking. We lost the game. We lost it **big** time, 14–88.

On the _____, Coach says, "What can I say? You are all a big problem. What is it going to take to get you to play like a team? What about _____?"

We do not _____ back to Coach. He gets the bus going. It is night. All I want is to get home fast. My little sister, B.J., is sick. I did not want to come to the _____ at all, but Mom wanted me to come. She says I have to keep going. I can't think about my _____ all the time.

"Forget the team," Tom says. "I can't wait to get on a college team. Then I can play with big-time _____."

I want to laugh. Tom is not going to get on a _____ team.

My friend Jake says to Tom, "**You** are the one who lost the game."

"What are you talking about?" Tom says. "**You** _____ the game. I'm the fastest _____ on the team."

Tom likes to talk big. "Forget it," I say.

"The _____ is," Tom goes on, "—the problem is the girl."

66

Name: _____ Date: _____

"I'm **Kate**, not **the girl**," Kate says, "and I'm the one who hit 4-for-4!"

The _____ does not have a girls' team. Kate gets to play on the boys' team.

"Girls can't play on this team," Tom says. Tom screams all the time. I don't think he is happy.

"Come off it," Jen says. "Tom, you are not _____ about the game. Don't take it out on Kate."

Jen doesn't play on the team. She works for us. She gets us drinks. She keeps the bus clean. She _____ a lot for us.

"Kate does help the team," I say to Tom. "She hit 4-for-4 in the game. What did you _____? I think it was 1-for-24."

"Forget you," Tom says. Then he talks to Jake. "I think Dan likes Kate."

Jake and Tom laugh at me.

"I do not," I say.

I **do** like Kate, but I am not _____ to say it to Jake and Tom.

Name: _____ Date: _____

B. Write the correct words on the lines to complete the sentences.

1. My dad is _____ a lot of money in his new job.

   | make | makes | making |

2. If I hear that one more time, I think I will _____.

   | scream | screams | scared |

3. That _____ is the biggest in class.

   | kid | kids | kidding |

4. My _____ helped me put out the _____ in my car.

   | find | fire | friend |

5. Kate sees her new _____ on the _____ the night of the game.

   | school | bus | boyfriend |

6. Jake is _____ his bike in the _____ at home.

   | hall | house | keeping |

7. Jake was sick and out of school for _____ and has to make up a lot of _____.

   | work | friend | days |

8. I think she is in my _____, but her sister is _____.

   | part | not | class |

9. Jen is going to have a big _____ selling her _____.

   | money | truck | problem |

10. I think Jake's little sister is _____ of big _____.

    | dogs | happy | scared |

68

Name: _____ Date: _____

C. Put words together from the box to make six new words. Write the new words in the blanks below.

boy	out	in	to	with	for
fire	drive	get	way	friend	truck

_____ _____

_____ _____

_____ _____

D. Use one of the new words you wrote to complete each sentence.

1. Jake is Jen's _____.

2. Did you _____ to come to school?

3. Jen is not home. We will go _____ her.

4. Who is driving the _____?

5. We can get _____ the car.

6. The car is in the _____.

E. Read the base words. Add an ending to make a new word.

Base Word	s	ed	ing
1. kid	_____	_____	_____
2. play	_____	_____	_____
3. stop	_____	_____	_____
4. fire	_____	_____	_____
5. call	_____	_____	_____

Name: _____ Date: _____

F. Circle the words that have the same ending as the first word. Then choose a word you circled to fill in the blank.

team	1.	seam	deep	dream	scream

I don't like when you _____ at me.

night	2.	bright	sight	light	bike

The _____ is out in my truck.

keep	3.	sleep	team	deep	street

I will go home and go to _____.

mad	4.	ad	fat	had	glad

I took out an _____ to sell the truck.

bike	5.	like	spike	hike	bright

I'm going for a _____ in the woods.

take	6.	back	sake	cake	make

We _____ a big fire in the woods.

all	7.	fall	stall	call	walk

We can't _____ you at night.

walk	8.	hall	hawk	talk	chalk

We wait by the fire and have a _____.

say	9.	stay	way	wall	pay

We can't _____ you for the car.

got	10.	spot	hot	cot	shop

The fire is _____.

Name: _____ Date: _____

MIDWAY ASSESSMENT LEVEL 2

A. Use the words in the box to fill in the blanks. Use each word one time.

over	teller	others	up	about
where	bank	finding	painting	principal
cold	There	longer	made	way

The kids have a problem waiting for Saturday because they want to know about the big play. That day Jared, Tom, Jen, Kate, and the _____ get to school at 9:00.

"I see we are _____ and at it," says Jen.

"I, for one, feel like a truck hit me," says Kate, "but I **did** make it on time."

They see Principal Walls in the hall. "Just the kids I want to see!" the _____ says. "Come with me." They go into a class where Mrs. Newman is waiting and wait just a little _____ for other kids to come. After a little time goes by, Mrs. Newman talks about the play.

"This is a play about a painter who wants to make people happy with his work," says Mr. Newman. "A girl sees him _____ day after day and goes out of her _____ to walk by to see how his work is coming. She does not look happy, and the painter wants to make her laugh."

The teacher goes on, "She and the painter get to be friends. But then it gets _____ out, and she no longer comes. The painter does not know _____ the girl is or what to do to go about _____ her. He thinks she does not have a home and may be cold. What will she do? How will she hold on?"

The kids like the play and can't wait to try out for parts. _____ is a shopkeeper, a cop, and a _____ at a bank, but the big parts are the painter and the lost girl. One by one, Principal Walls and Mrs. Newman work with the kids to see who will play which part.

Name: _____ Date: _____

After they try out, Principal Walls and Mrs. Newman go into a class to talk it _____. The kids wait.

"Who do you think they will find for the painter?" says Tom.

"I don't think I will get the part of the lost girl," says Kate.

"Maybe," Jen says, "but **I'm** the one who didn't know what to say!"

"What _____ you, Jared?" Kate says. "How did you do?"

"A bad job, for the most part," says Jared, "so it looks like the painter may go to anyone."

They wait and wait for the principal and Mrs. Newman to come back out. Then the big news: "Kids, Mrs. Newman and I have _____ Jared our painter, and Jen the lost girl. Kate is the _____ teller, Jake is the shopkeeper, and Tom is the cop."

Jen is so happy she screams. Kate did want to be the lost girl, but she is happy for Jen. Jared, Tom, and Jake are laughing.

B. Circle the words that have the same ending as the first word. Then choose a word you circled to fill in the blank.

say	1. pay	rake	play	may
	I _____ go to the game on Saturday.			
hall	2. walk	wall	tall	call
	A _____ man painted the graffiti.			
cook	3. took	moon	coach	book
	Kate _____ me to see the principal.			
tell	4. ten	sell	bell	well
	Jared will not _____ his car.			

Name: _____ Date: _____

ad   5. **Dad**   after   **bad**   **mad**

Kate had a _____ feeling about the ring.

stop   6. **shop**   **pop**   **start**   **crop**

Kate will sell the ring at the _____.

sold   7. **hold**   **cold**   **call**   **fold**

Can you _____ this money for me?

back   8. **bake**   **pack**   **rack**   **tack**

You can put the money in your _____.

C. Read each base word. Add an ending to make a new word. If the ending does not make a new word, leave the line blank.

Base Word	s	ed	ing	en	ly
1. light	_____	_____	_____	_____	_____
2. wood	_____	_____	_____	_____	_____
3. friend	_____	_____	_____	_____	_____
4. clean	_____	_____	_____	_____	_____
5. put	_____	_____	_____	_____	_____

Name: _____ Date: _____

FINAL ASSESSMENT LEVEL 2

A. Use the words in the box to fill in the blanks. Use each word one time.

backpacks	idea	paint	bags	know
shop	bosses	mad	sleeping	call
mountain	talking	field	next	working

I race my _____ bike to my job. I work in a shop called Mountain Works. We sell backpacks, _____ bags, and mountain bikes. Dan and Kay Ramos own Mountain Works. They are my _____.

I put my bike in the back of the shop. When I walk into the _____, Dan Ramos starts in on me. "What's your problem? I wanted you to put the backpacks on the wall by the window."

"Sorry," I say, "I'll put them on the wall."

"Forget it," he says. "I'm going to paint that wall. Just put the _____ over there."

What is his problem? One idea one day, the next day another _____. Is this going to be a bad day? I get to work with the backpacks. I don't like Dan Ramos. He is on me all the time. But I work hard because the money is good. I try not to make him _____.

"Dan?" Kay Ramos calls from the back of the shop. "A call for you."

I keep working with the backpacks. But as I go by the back of the shop, I hear Dan Ramos say, "I have him. I'll keep him _____. He makes $120 a week. Where will he go?" Then I hear Dan Ramos laugh. "Not a problem," he says. Then he stops talking. The _____ is over.

74

Name: _____   Date: _____

He is _____ about me! Who is he talking to? My mom? My dad? I don't think they ever call the Ramoses.

He comes out of the back.

"Do you know that kid, Mike Day?" he asks me.

"I _____ him."

"Good ballplayer, I hear."

What does Dan Ramos want to know about Mike for? "He is good in the _____," I say, "and he can really hit."

Dan Ramos smiles. Then he says, "What are you looking at? You have a lot to do. Get at it."

"Sorry," I say, but I want to hit him. "What do you want me to do _____?"

"Put some of the new sleeping _____ in the window. Make it look good. After that, I want you to paint the back of the shop."

I look at the time. I don't have time to _____ the back of the shop. He does that all the time. He gives me work I can't do in the time I have. I'll just have to get started on it.

Dan and Kay Ramos go home at 5:00 when the shop closes. That is when I start painting the back.

I keep thinking about that call. I keep thinking about Ramos talking about me and my job.

Name: _____ Date: _____

B. Write the correct words on the lines to complete each sentence.

1. Dan and Kay Ramos are my _____.

   | boss   bosses   friends |

2. In the shop, they sell sleeping bags, _____, and mountain bikes.

   | backpack   backpacks   windows |

3. Dan is talking to someone, but I don't know _____ it is.

   | what   when   who |

4. Dan wanted to know about Mike, so I told him that Mike was a good _____.

   | field   ballplayer   friend |

5. He told me to paint the back of the shop, but I don't have time for _____ now.

   | call   paint   painting |

6. I don't think I am _____ at work.

   | scared   happy   like |

7. I want to know who Dan was talking to _____ me.

   | for   about   with |

8. I work in the shop because I make good money, but _____ Dan makes me so mad I want to hit him.

   | one   sometimes   like |

9. I have more work to do in the shop, but there is time to do it after the shop _____ at 5:00.

   | stop   wait   closes |

10. There is a lot about Dan and Kay Ramos that I don't really _____.

    | like   care   feel |

76

Name: _____ Date: _____

C. Write the correct words on the lines to complete each sentence.

1. My Mom and Dad got _____ on a Saturday.
   | marries   marrying   married |

2. Jen is _____ to us from the boat.
   | waved   waving   wave |

3. Jared _____ know the boat has been smashed.
   | doesn't   don't   what's |

4. We went to some _____ at the new school.
   | class's   classes   class |

5. Our team won the _____.
   | champion   teamwork   championship |

6. My dad has the _____ boat I have ever seen.
   | biggest   bigger   big |

7. I can run _____ than my sister.
   | fastest   faster   fast |

8. My boat is _____.
   | wood   wooden   woods |

9. Jen is _____ with the new kids at school.
   | friends   friend   friendly |

10. The boy and his family are _____.
    | homes   homework   homeless |

D. Circle the words that have the same ending as the first word. Then choose a word you circled to fill in the blank.

shop   1. stop   hop   cop   rob
I want you to _____ the truck now.

back   2. pack   bad   sack   rack
I put the bags on the car _____.

sold   3. hold   gold   fold   stop
The ring is made of _____.

and   4. band   fan   sand   grand
The _____ plays if the team wins the game.

77

Name: _____ Date: _____

MIDWAY ASSESSMENT LEVEL 3

A. Use the words in the box to fill in the blanks. Use each word one time.

another	down	job	mind	ship
anything	family	kitchen	almost	shop
doesn't	herself	know	really	time

"I don't see how you keep from going out of your _____ here, Will," she tells him. "It's a madhouse, and I don't ever see you sit _____!"

"Are you kidding?" says Will. "This job at Graffiti is the best job I have!" He packs _____ three orders, and then he calls again, "Order up!" A family of three comes over to get their dinner. Inez waits as Will rings them up.

When the _____ goes back and sits down, she asks, "Are you telling me you hold down more than one _____?"

Will stops what he is doing and looks at Inez. *These Robin's Beach girls!* he thinks. But then he sees that she really does want to _____. "Yes, Inez, I do," he tells her.

"But you are here _____ every time I come in," says Inez. "When do you find time to work another job?"

Will laughs. "Inez," he says, "with my schoolwork and Graffiti, I don't really **find** time for _____!" Again he looks over at the dinners that are cooking. "I make time," he says, coming back.

"Why?" she wants to know.

"Well, we lost my mom some _____ ago," Will says.

"I'm so sorry," Inez says, and in her mind she is mad at _____ for asking. But Will sees how she feels.

"It's OK," he tells her. "But my dad is having a hard time. And there isn't any work for him in these parts right now. He _____ needs my help to make ends meet."

"Do you mind if I ask what else you do?" Inez asks.

Name: _____ Date: _____

"Well, on weekends I work in a _____ by the beach," Will says.

"Doing what?"

"I pack fish," Will says, "and _____ them all over the U.S."

"Fish?" says Inez. "I guess that **does** make Graffiti the better job, then!" Will is cleaning the _____ as they talk. Inez gives him a long, long look. She _____ know many kids in Robin's Beach who work **one** job, and here Will Cruz holds down **two**! *How does he do it?* she thinks.

B. Circle the words that have the same ending as the first word. Then choose a word you circled to fill in the blank.

hit 1. fit   fight   sit   quit

Jake _____ the baseball team.

name 2. game   same   shame   ham

Jared has taken Jake's place in the _____.

light 3. bright   sight   lit   night

The mountains are tall. They are a _____ to see!

old 4. gold   shop   cold   told

I _____ my mom about the graffiti.

face 5. grace   lace   place   fast

Coach saved a _____ for Carmen on the team.

find 6. mind   wind   fit   climb

Do you _____ if I stop here?

should 7. cold   could   wood   would

Tom _____ like to try out for the team too.

better 8. letter   setter   go-getter   best

I will give the _____ to my sister at the baseball game.

Name: _____ Date: _____

C. Read each base word. Add an ending to make a new word. If the ending does not make a new word, leave the line blank.

Base Word	s	es	ed	er	ing
1. box	_____	_____	_____	_____	_____
2. pass	_____	_____	_____	_____	_____
3. place	_____	_____	_____	_____	_____
4. face	_____	_____	_____	_____	_____
5. point	_____	_____	_____	_____	_____

Name: _____ Date: _____

FINAL ASSESSMENT LEVEL 3

A. Use the words in the box to fill in the blanks. Use each word one time.

again	forget	sister	clean	homework
something	cooking	outside	trying	doesn't
points	where	down	sale	why

"I'm off to an apartment sale," says Carmen.

"Don't you have _____?" says her mom.

"I did it, Mom."

"What about your room?" says her sister Inez. "You said you would _____ your room."

"Oh, Inez! Get off my back," says Carmen.

"Carmen! Don't talk to your _____ that way," says her mom. "Did you clean your room?"

"No—but Mom! I want to get to this _____ before all the good things are gone. Can't I clean my room when I get back?"

"OK," says her mom, "but don't _____."

"No way." Carmen moves to the door. But then she runs into her grandma.

"_____ are you going, Carmen?" the old woman wants to know. "Don't you want dinner?"

"It's only 3:30!" Carmen _____ out. "I'll be back long before dinner time."

"OK, but don't forget," says her grandma. "I'm _____ something just for you."

"I'll be here." Carmen has now made it all the way to the hall. But Inez runs after her. "Carmen! Can I come, too?"

81

Name: _____ Date: _____

"No," says Carmen. "_____ do you even ask?"

"Mom! Carmen is being mean to me again!"

"No, Inez," says their mom. "Carmen has a right to go places without you."

Just then, Cougar, the dog, races through the hall. He has _____ in his mouth.

"Your dog has my homework!" cries Inez.

"**My** dog? Cougar is **your** dog, too!"

"No, he is not. He is your dog! Your name starts with 'C'. He is your dog. He has my homework! Do something!"

"Put it _____, boy!" Carmen screams at the dog. But Cougar runs away from her fast.

"Get my homework back!" Inez screams.

"I'm _____," says Carmen, as she moves closer to the dog. But Cougar knows what she is up to. He takes off. Carmen lets him go. Cougar has a dog door. He can get _____ on his own. That homework is as good as gone. No one will ever see it again. Inez will have to do it over.

Then she hears Inez say, "Oh! Here is my homework after all. The dog didn't get it. That must have been Carmen's homework. Carmen! You have to do your homework over _____!"

Carmen thinks, *I better get out while I can.* She opens the door.

"Carmen!" her mom calls out. But Carmen _____ hear her. Carmen is outside at last. She is already on her way to the bus stop.

82

Name: _____ Date: _____

B. Write the words on the lines that correctly complete each sentence.

1. Carmen doesn't want to clean her room because she wants to go to a _____.

   | game | sale | apartment |

2. Carmen's _____, Inez, wants to go with Carmen.

   | mom | grandma | sister |

3. Carmen's mom told her she could _____ her room when she got back.

   | try | clean | leave |

4. Grandma is going to cook something just for Carmen for _____.

   | kitchen | homework | dinner |

5. Mom told Inez she could not go with Carmen because Carmen had the right to go places by _____.

   | school | herself | himself |

6. Inez says that Cougar has her _____.

   | card | sale | homework |

7. Inez doesn't think that Cougar is her _____ because her name starts with 'I'.

   | grandma | homework | dog |

8. When Cougar wants to go _____, he goes out his own dog door.

   | inside | outside | over |

9. Carmen is the one who went after Cougar to _____ the homework from him.

   | help | get | give |

10. Carmen is going to take a _____ to the apartment sale.

    | bus | car | truck |

C. Find words in the puzzle that have the same endings as the words in the box. Words can go across, down, or diagonally. Circle each word and write it on the line. There is one word match for each word in the box.

could	had	gold	tame	hot	tile
find	cook	just	save	guy	face
wet	hit	night	letter	fast	bell

X	N	A	M	E	M	U	S	T	U
S	A	T	O	O	K	S	S	Y	O
I	O	P	L	A	S	T	H	S	S
G	L	G	L	Y	O	M	O	A	O
H	O	A	A	F	L	I	U	D	B
T	P	F	C	V	D	L	L	T	U
C	O	I	I	E	E	E	D	E	Y
L	T	T	W	I	N	D	A	L	P
P	O	O	R	Y	S	E	T	L	P
B	E	T	T	E	R	L	A	C	E

should   sad   sold   name

pot   mile   wind   took

must   gave   buy   lace

set   fit   sight   better

last   tell

Name: _____ Date: _____

MIDWAY ASSESSMENT LEVEL 4

A. Use the words in the box to fill in the blanks. Use each word one time.

beach	clean	maybe	name	problems
being	different	memory	pointing	raced
belongs	good	monster	pretty	someone

"Now, you just sit down here, Ty, and I'll get you something cold to drink," says Grandma Inez. "Those boats can really turn you inside out when you aren't used to them."

"My _____ is **Tyrone**, and I'm OK."

"Well, **you** can call **me** Gran," she tells him with a smile, "and, if you don't mind my saying so, your face still looks _____ green for someone who's 'OK.'" Without another word, she goes into the kitchen and comes back with two cold drinks. "Try this," she says, sitting down next to him.

Tyrone looks at this woman who is his grandmother. "You know, I really didn't want to come here," he says, thinking he sounds like a _____, but too mad to care.

"And I hope it makes you feel better to say it." Gran smiles. "But you **are** here, and that makes it _____." Gran gets up and goes to the window. "The time will fly by! You'll see. It's just that—well, right now your mom and dad have some things to work out."

"What you **mean** is that they want me out of the picture," says Tyrone. "I was in the way." The _____ is hard. Tyrone finds that, for the first time in a long time, he feels like crying.

85

Name: _____ Date: _____

"No, no, you're wrong about that," says Grandma Inez. "But they **do** need some time together. And, in the meantime, I'm really happy to have you here with me on Spider's Point. It will be _____ for all of us."

Good for you, maybe, Tyrone thinks. *Me, I'm out of here.* He gets up and walks over to the fireplace to look at the pictures on the wall.

"That's your dad," says Gran, _____ to one of the pictures, "when he was a little boy."

"You're kidding," says Tyrone. It's hard to believe his dad was ever a kid. But there he is, down at the beach, with a big smile on his face.

"Not at all," says Gran. "He was on his boat, the *Venus Light*, in that picture right after he won a big race."

"Dad _____ boats when he was a kid?" Tyrone can't picture it.

"All the time," Gran says with a smile. "Of course, he gave it up when he moved away."

"Did boats make him sick too?" asks Tyrone.

"Oh, no," laughs Gran. "He was used to _____ on a boat, Ty. It was all I could do to get him to come in for dinner! He wanted to be out on the water from sunup to sundown!"

"Forget that!" says Tyrone. "I like my dinner **in** me, where it _____." Gran just laughs at that. He turns to her. "Where is the boat now?" Tyrone wants to know.

86

"The *Venus Light*? Still out back, under the beach house, believe it or not," says Gran, "—just waiting for a boy like you to _____ her up and get her going again."

Tyrone gives his grandmother a long look. "You would let me do that?" he asks at last. "That is—if I wanted to?"

"Well, I would have to get _____ to show you how, of course," she answers, "but that's no problem."

Tyrone just can't believe it. She would let him use the *Venus Light*! If she's right about boats not **always** making you sick, then maybe his time on Spider's Point won't be so bad after all! But, then again, it's been a long time, and _____ that boat is just a lot of old wood now. "When can I see it?" he asks.

"Just as fast as your legs will take you, Ty," laughs Gran. "Go outside, turn to the _____, and look under the seaside end of the house. She's been waiting for you."

Gran smiles after Tyrone as he races out of the house. *He's had so many _____ at home*, she thinks. *Being at Spider's Point is just the thing to put some life and hope back into that boy!* She walks out behind him to see his face as he finds the *Venus Light*. Tyrone's eyes turn into big circles.

Yes, Ty, she says to herself with a smile, *the sea is calling your name.*

Name: _____ Date: _____

B. Write the word or words on the line that will correctly complete each sentence.

1. | happy   mad   sick |

    Ty was feeling _____ from being in a boat.

2. | time   problems   ideas |

    Ty came to live with his grandma because his mom and dad had some _____ they needed to work out.

3. | happy   sad   mad |

    He was not _____ about coming to stay with Grandma.

4. | school   way   woods |

    Because his mom and dad want Ty to live with his grandma, Ty feels they just want him out of the _____.

5. | race   make   look at |

    When Ty's dad was a kid and used to live on Spider's Point, he had a boat that he liked to _____.

6. | clean it up   get it going   name the boat |

    Grandma thinks Ty will need help with the *Venus Light*. She tells him that he will need someone else to show him how to _____ _____.

7. | water   beach   house |

    Dad's old boat has been under the _____ for many years.

8. | mad at   sorry for   like screaming |

    Grandma feels _____ Ty.

Name: _____ Date: _____

9. | right   wrong   same |

When Ty sees the *Venus Light* and Grandma sees his face, she knows she has done the _____ thing by telling him to look at the boat.

10. | keep   like   mind |

Because Ty has the *Venus Light*, he may not _____ his time at Grandma's so much.

C. Write three sentences telling what you would do if you had an old boat like Ty's.

_____
_____
_____
_____
_____
_____
_____
_____
_____
_____
_____

FINAL ASSESSMENT LEVEL 4

A. Use the words in the box to fill in the blanks. Use each word one time.

computer	home	mind	other	spaceship
eyes	interested	night	own	trying
happens	make	nothing	problem	yourself

The ship has been out in space for two days. No one is scared anymore. They have a new _____ now. They have nothing to do. They feel too pushed together. There isn't much room on the _____.

"Do you have to sit there?" Jake asks Kate. He gives her a mean look.

"Why not?" She throws the look right back at him. "You don't _____ this place. I have every right to sit anywhere I want."

"Kids, kids," says Mu Lan with a laugh. She is _____ to get them to lighten up.

"Who are you to call us kids?" says Kate. "What gives you the right to talk down to us?"

"I didn't mean it that way!" Mu Lan cries.

Tyrone has said _____ so far. He is sitting in the darkest corner of the spaceship. He is caught up in what he's doing.

Kate goes back there to be with him. "I have had it with them," she says. "Talk and fight, day and _____. I can't stand them! Yet, I like them, really. It's just that this ship is too small. How do you do it, Tyrone?"

90

Name: _____   Date: _____

"Do what?" He does not take his _____ off his computer.

"Put up with us! We are only two days into this trip, and already I feel like I want to go _____. But you, Tyrone, nothing seems to get to you. What do you know that we don't? How come you hardly ever say anything?"

"I have nothing to say," Tyrone answers. "Anyway, Kate, I have to keep my _____ on this thing."

"What thing? What is this work you're doing now?"

"This is not work, Kate. I am playing a game."

"A game?" says Kate. "A _____ game?"

"Yes, like the ones kids play down on Earth," Tyrone answers.

"You're just a big kid _____, aren't you?" says Kate.

"Well, I do like computer games," says Tyrone. His hands are moving fast. Kate sees lights moving in the computer.

"What's going on?" she asks.

"Well, right now—" But just then something bad _____ in the game. He cries out, "Oh!" Then he laughs and sits back. "Well, I lost. Really, you should try this game," he smiles. "It will keep your mind off _____ things, Kate."

"Maybe we should all try them," she says. "These games could save us." She calls to the other two. "Mu Lan! Jake! Come here. Look at what Tyrone has."

91

Mu Lan does not seem _____. "A computer? What about it?"

"It's not just a computer. Tyrone has some games here."

"I'm not into computer games," says Mu Lan.

"I am," says Jake. "Is this a good one? What is it?"

"I call it **Over the Mountain**," says Tyrone. "But if you don't like this one, I have others."

"What do you mean, **you call it**?" Kate asks. "Did you make it up?"

"Yes. That's one of the things I do," says Tyrone. "I _____ up computer games."

"You're a man of many parts," says Mu Lan.

"He's really just a big boy," says Kate. It's not hard to see that she likes Tyrone.

"There is a little boy in every man," says Jake. "Move over, Tyrone. I'll take a turn at this game. Show me how to play."

Name: _____ Date: _____

B. Write the word or words on the line that will correctly complete each sentence.

1. | scared   happy   sick |

   When they were first out in space, Mu Lan, Jake, Tyrone, and Kate were _____.

2. | the Earth   each other   the sun |

   It seems that the people on the spaceship feel that they are too close to _____.

3. | anything   nothing   something |

   Kate thinks that _____ seems to get to Tyrone.

4. | problems   sickness   work |

   Tyrone keeps his mind off his _____ by playing a computer game.

5. | Kate   Jake   Mu Lan |

   Everyone but _____ seems interested in the computer game.

6. | good at   studying for   tired of |

   It seems that Tyrone is _____ making up computer games.

7. | being so tired   feeling pushed together   being mad at everyone |

   Kate seems to think that the computer games could keep them all from _____.

8. | wanting to be alone   trying to make games   good at many things |

   When Mu Lan tells Tyrone that he is a man of many parts, she means that he is _____.

Name: _____ Date: _____

9. | find work   get along   make games |

   If they are all in a small spaceship, it could be a real problem if they don't all _____.

10. | make the games   pass the time   talk to Mu Lan |

    It seems that they may have found a way to _____.

C. Write three sentences telling what you would do if you were in a small spaceship with three other people.

_____
_____
_____
_____
_____
_____
_____
_____
_____
_____

Name: _____ Date: _____

MIDWAY ASSESSMENT LEVEL 5

A. Use the words in the box to fill in the blanks. Use each word one time.

ahead	believed	count	remembers	sound
anything	bills	family	screamed	weeks
answer	blanket	known	someday	wrong

Dad had just come home from working in the mine, Mom was cooking dinner, and Carmen had been helping the boys with their schoolwork. The family was happy, Carmen _____. The mining was going well. Gold had hit its highest point in history! Everyone said it was going to make for a new South America, a new way of life! And César Cruz, Carmen's dad, had _____ it.

Talk that not everyone was happy did not scare César Cruz. "Those men will see!" he would laugh. "When the money comes in, and they can pay the _____, and there are no more sharecroppers, **then** they will come around! It will be fine, little Carmen," Dad would say. "It will all work out."

"Oh, Dad!" Carmen had said. "I am not a little girl! I am 16 years old now!"

"You are **my** 16-year-old little girl, then!" Dad had laughed. "And _____ you will be 26, and 36, and 46 years old. Even then," Dad had said, "you will be my little girl."

Carmen smiles at the memory. It seems like it was only a day or two ago, but it was really 13 or 14 _____ back—a lifetime. Carmen doesn't know if it is the night or the cold memory that moves her, but she gets out the only thing she owns in the camp—a small cloth _____—and pulls it around herself.

Name: _____ Date: _____

Again, her mind goes back to that night. *It will be fine, little Carmen,* Dad had said. But he had been _____. For the first time in her life, Carmen saw that César Cruz could be wrong. Things would **not** be OK. In fact, after that night, things would never be OK again.

Is there _____ that could have been different? Mom had still been cooking dinner when the men came. Dad had been talking to the boys, so Carmen had put their schoolwork aside. But as she stood up, she and Mom had heard a _____.

"What was that?" Carmen's mom had asked.

"I didn't hear anything," said Dad, who was telling the boys a joke.

Again, there were small sounds. Then bigger sounds. Then people calling out!

Carmen remembers Dad laughing. "I think the boys from the mine have started to _____ their money a little too fast! It sounds like they have been drinking their pay!"

But no one was laughing at what happened next. A man had hit the door three times, calling out, "Open up! Open up right now!" Before the _____ could even move, two other men hit the door so hard that it crashed down.

"What is this?!" cried César Cruz, who stood up fast. He pushed the boys behind him and put out his hand for Carmen.

"Is your name Cruz? **César** Cruz?" the men asked.

96

Name: _____ Date: _____

"Who wants to know?" Carmen's dad came back. But they had not liked that _____, not at all, so they hit Carmen's dad over the head so hard that it had thrown him on the ground. "Take him!" one of the men had ordered. "Take them **all** out with the others!"

Carmen's mom then _____ as man after man had come into their home, where they had always been safe, and pulled them all outside.

There, in the night, Carmen had seen people being pushed to the field where she and her friends played stickball every day. And over in that field Carmen heard screams that said life as they had _____ it was over. *What was going to happen to them all?* she wanted to know. Then, somehow, she knew.

"Run!" she called out in a bold move. "Run for your lives!" With that, Carmen had pulled free of a man who had his hands on her arm, and she raced for the woods. "Run!" she screamed again and again as she raced, scared to look back and even more scared of what was _____. For miles and miles, Carmen screamed and ran.

Thinking back on it, Carmen can't believe she got away that night. But remembering is hard, and she shakes her head as if that could make the memory go away. She sits on the hard earth in camp, her eyes moving over the tents, the people, and the ruin of the place she now calls home. At last, she looks back up to the sky. *I will go on*, she says to herself. *Like the stars, I will go on.*

Name: _____ Date: _____

B. Write the word or words on the line that will correctly complete each sentence.

1. | shop   mine   school |

   Carmen's father worked in a _____.

2. | California   Africa   South America |

   The Cruz family lived in _____.

3. | gold   cars   college |

   Mr. Cruz thinks that _____ would help sharecroppers make a new life.

4. | woods   dogs   sounds |

   Before the men came to the Cruzes' door, there were _____ outside.

5. | her house   the field   the woods |

   Carmen got away and ran to hide in _____.

6. | ordering   remembering   asking |

   Carmen is in some kind of camp, _____ what happened to her and her family.

7. | likes a lot   does not like   will leave today |

   The camp must be a place Carmen _____.

8. | play   leave   live |

   She doesn't know what will happen to her, but Carmen knows she will _____.

Name: _____ Date: _____

C. Write three sentences telling what you would do if you were living in a camp without your family like Carmen.

1. _____

   _____

   _____

2. _____

   _____

   _____

3. _____

   _____

   _____

Name: _____   Date: _____

FINAL ASSESSMENT LEVEL 5

A. Use the words in the box to fill in the blanks. Use each word one time.

already	hall	meeting	safe	talking
even	homework	news	school	understands
finish	last	people	someday	would

Mom gets home from work at 6:00. We turn on the TV and eat dinner from a can. She doesn't feel like cooking. Most days, I cook dinner. But I feel really bad tonight. The way Mrs. Well talked to me makes me want to die.

Mom never gets mad at me when I don't make dinner. She _____ that some days you just can't do everything right. She doesn't ask any questions. We just eat out of a can and look at the news.

Mom and I look at the _____ every night. We want to see if any Americans go off to fight somewhere. We don't want Levi to have to do any real fighting.

There is more to why I like to look at the news. **No one** knows this. But _____ I'd like to be the woman who reads the news on TV.

I know. You have to go to college to do that. So I'll never get to have that job. But even so, sometimes when Inez Ramos is doing the news, I think about what it _____ be like if that was me.

I don't tell Mom about having to stay after school. I feel so scared about what Mrs. Well said. I might not even _____ high school. What will I do then?

100

Name: _____ Date: _____

The thing is, the more scared I feel, the harder it is to do my _____. When I get scared, I can't think. Maybe I just will not go to school the next day. Mom would kill me.

Then I remember that first thing the next day is an all-school meeting. I can do my homework as the meeting is going on. This thought makes me feel better. After the news, I go to sleep.

I can't believe it! Who do I see first thing the next day in school but Mrs. Well. She is walking down the _____ toward me. I act as if I don't see her. She is just going to ask if I did my homework.

"Wilma," she stops me in the hall, "you're going the wrong way," she says. "The all-school meeting is this way."

I can't tell her I'm missing the all-school meeting to do my homework. So I have to turn around and walk with her to the _____. I try to find a place to sit away from her. But she sits down right next to me. I want to die.

The principal, Mr. Swimmer, gets up to talk. He says, "I have some bad news. This is the _____ year Rivet High School will be open. Next year, each of you will have to take a bus to another school."

What? All the kids start _____ at the same time. You would think the high school closing would make me happy. I can get out of this place at last. But I feel scared. Another high school? I have enough problems trying to stay in this one. I'm used to Rivet High.

Mr. Swimmer goes on. "This building is not _____. The city doesn't want us to be here another year. Too much needs to be fixed on the building, and there just isn't any money to do it. So the head of the city's schools, Mr. Singer, has ordered us out. We talked him into letting us finish out the school year."

I look at Mrs. Well. I can tell she has _____ heard this news. Her face is hard and mad-looking. Will she lose her job?

Some kids start laughing. But I feel as if someone has just hit me. First, they say there is no money for the one thing about school I liked—band. Now they say there is no money for our school at all.

_____ talk about kids not caring about school. One can't like school if there aren't enough books. In science class, there is only one book for every three kids. It's hard to do the work when I don't _____ have my own book. Now they are saying they can't even keep the school open.

Why should I do my homework if they can't even get enough books or schools?

Right then, I know what I'm going to do. I'm going to leave _____. After all, Mrs. Well said I was not going to make it anyway. I'll get a job. Maybe I'll join the Navy like Levi.

I don't care. I don't care about anything.

Name: _____ Date: _____

B. Write the phrase on the line that will correctly complete each sentence.

1. | made her feel scared
   | made her mom happy
   | made Mrs. Well feel friendly

   Wilma had a meeting with Mrs. Well that _____

   _____.

2. | an office worker
   | a newswoman
   | at school more

   It seems that Wilma would like to be _____.

3. | cooks dinner
   | eats out
   | opens cans

   Most days, Wilma _____.

4. | looks at TV
   | is eating
   | can't think

   Wilma doesn't do her homework one night because she

   _____.

5. | away in the Navy
   | at Rivet High School
   | gone for the day

   Wilma and her mom care a lot about Levi, who is not with them

   because he is _____.

Name: _____ Date: _____

6. | some problems
   | Mrs. Well
   | Mr. Swimmer

Wilma tried to miss the all-school meeting, but she ended up going because she ran into _____.

7. | there weren't enough kids who wanted to go to the school
   | there wasn't enough money to fix all the things that were wrong
   | there weren't enough books for everyone to have

The city wanted to close Rivet High School because

_____

_____.

8. | have to take a bus to another school
   | not get to finish high school
   | have to get jobs or go into the Navy

When the school is closed, the kids from Rivet High School will

_____.

9. | tells the kids at Rivet High School that he has bad news
   | talked Mr. Singer into leaving the school open to finish the school year
   | thinks Mrs. Well may lose her job

It seems Mr. Swimmer doesn't want to close Rivet High School right away because he _____

_____.

10. | not been a good place to go to school
    | a principal who doesn't care about kids
    | had money problems for some time

From what you have read, you can tell that Rivet High School has

_____.

Name: _____ Date: _____

C. Write three sentences telling what you would do if your school were going to close and you would have to go somewhere else.

1. _____

   _____

   _____

2. _____

   _____

   _____

3. _____

   _____

   _____

MIDWAY ASSESSMENT LEVEL 6

A. Use the words in the box to fill in the blanks. Use each word one time.

around	doesn't	little	something
starts	band	glass	song
street	joke	stairs	

Cruz looks back at Mike, who is setting the beat with his sticks. Cruz points up, letting him know that this is the last song for the night. Mike shakes his head up and down—*Got you, Cruz*—before the _____ lets go with a _____ from their new CD called, "Leaving You." The fans go mad! They scream! They cry! They pass out! *It just _____ get any better than this*, thinks Cruz.

As the song comes to an end, Mike throws his sticks up into the air, and the band takes in the screams of 30,000 people.

"Can you believe it?" laughs Mike as they head back to the bus that is waiting for them. They can still hear the screaming people calling out, "More! More! More!"

"There were three girls who made it up the _____ before the police stopped them!" says Cruz. "I stood there thinking, 'Where are the cops? Where are the cops?'"

"And did you see that guy?" asks Ana, who sings backup. "The one the policeman took out?" She shakes her head. "I don't know—there was _____ about him that gave me a bad feeling."

Name: _____ Date: _____

There are 10 people in the band, and most of them get on the bus, but Mike and Cruz head to Mike's car parked close by. The next stop for the band will be an after-show dinner at Rhymes. "We'll meet you there," Mike and Cruz call out to the others. They get in the car and take off into the late California night.

Cruz puts his head back, closes his eyes, and _____ to sing their last song of the night in a low voice.

"Hey!" Mike calls out at the corner light. "Was anyone else going to Rhymes by car?"

"No, I don't think so," Cruz says. "Why?"

"Someone back there is coming up fast and moving from one side of the _____ to the other."

"What kind of car is it?" Cruz wants to know.

"I can't tell," says Mike. "But it looks a _____ like a green FX-7."

"Just let him pass," says Cruz, his eyes still closed.

"That's the thing," says Mike, still keeping an eye on the car behind them. "He doesn't seem to want to pass."

Cruz turns _____ to look back, just as the driver in the car behind them makes his move. "This guy is out of his mind!" cries Cruz. "He's going to hit us, Mike!"

107

Name: _____   Date: _____

"Look out!" screams Cruz as the FX-7 hits them and throws their car into two oncoming cars. Mike tries not to hit the other cars, and he runs the car up on a sidewalk and through the _____ window of a card shop.

Both Cruz and Mike are quiet for a little while after the car comes to a stop.

"Are you OK?" asks Cruz.

Mike's face looks white, but he says, "I'm all right."

The two of them get out of the car and look it over. "Not pretty," says Cruz. "Not pretty at all." Now that he knows they are all right, Cruz tries to make a _____ of it. "Of course," he adds, "it's not how I would have stopped a car, but I guess it worked."

"So next time," says Mike, his eyes on Cruz, "**you** drive."

Name: _____ Date: _____

B. Write the word on the line that correctly completes each sentence.

1. | words   song   act |

   The band's last _____ of the night is from the new CD.

2. | new   light   good |

   It seems that the people listening think that the band is very _____.

3. | problems   noise   break |

   There seem to be some _____ because the police had to take a guy away.

4. | talk   sing   eat |

   The band was going to meet after the show at Rhymes so the band

   members could _____.

5. | followed   changed   helpless |

   Cruz and Mike think that they are being _____.

Name: _____ Date: _____

C. Write the phrase on the line that correctly completes each sentence.

1. | she could see that the police were taking him away
   | there was just something about him
   | she knew him and didn't like him

   Ana had a bad feeling about one guy because _____
   _____.

2. | everyone got on the bus
   | some got on the bus and some got in the car
   | everyone but Mike got on the bus

   When they finished the show and were going to the restaurant, _____
   _____.

3. | Mike was driving
   | Mike was singing
   | Cruz was driving

   When they got in the car, _____
   _____.

4. | they should have stopped at the light and they didn't
   | a car was coming toward them and they didn't see it
   | they wanted to miss running into other cars

   Cruz and Mike ran through the glass in the shop because _____
   _____.

5. | wants to meet them
   | wants to hurt them
   | wants to drive their car

   It seems that there is someone who _____.

110

Name: _____ Date: _____

D. Write three sentences telling what you would do if you were a rock star like Cruz.

1. _____
_____
_____

2. _____
_____
_____

3. _____
_____
_____

E. Write three sentences telling what you think Cruz and Mike should do next.

1. _____
_____
_____

2. _____
_____
_____

3. _____
_____
_____

FINAL ASSESSMENT LEVEL 6

A. Use the words in the box to fill in the blanks. Use each word one time.

apart	guitar	name	something	doesn't
isn't	pick	song	door	jobs
read	stolen	follows	money	ready
think	guess	music	really	tonight

After dinner that night, Will picks up his guitar and heads down the street to see his friend, Robert.

"Hey, Will," says Robert as he opens the _____. "What's happening, man?"

"Nothing much. Same old," says Will. "You?"

"Sitting around with Jared and Mark. Come in."

"Oh, are they here, too?" Will _____ Robert down the stairs to his room. He waves to the other two. "What's happening, boys?"

"Meeting of the band?" Jared smiles.

The band is a joke with these guys. They all like _____, and for years now they have been getting together to play. But they just do it to have a good time. They know they're not _____ a band. Oh, they play for friends now and again. One time they played at a school social. But they have never played for people they don't know. Sometimes they joke about getting _____ as a band, but they know they are not good enough. Who would pay to hear them? Still the joke keeps coming up. These days, they sometimes forget to laugh.

112

Name: _____ Date: _____

"Jared is right," says Robert. "We're all here, and Will has his _____. Why don't we play some music? I was writing a song today. Does anyone want to hear it?"

"You?" laughs Jared.

"Why not me? I didn't say it was a **great song**, just a _____."

"Hey, that's cool, Robert," says Will. "Did you write down the words?"

"Sure did. Here. You guys _____ along as I sing it." Robert runs through his song a few times, and after that his friends join in. The song is about a girl. Will likes the feeling it gives. The words are sad, but in a good way. They make him _____ of Ana.

"You never see me at all,
Never know I'm there.
I love you more than all the world,
Girl—how come, how come you don't care?"

Yes, thinks Will. *That's just how it is. She _____ even know I'm there!* Suddenly his hands are on fire. He can turn his feelings right into music. He takes off on a guitar break. The other guys back him up, give him space, and let him burn. Soon Will is flying. At last, _____ tells him it is time to come back. He drives his guitar back to Earth and lands just where he took off. Robert has a big smile on his face, and his eyes are closed. He starts to sing again. A thought races through Will's mind. _____ *we **are** a band.*

Name: _____ Date: _____

When the song ends, no one says anything at first. Then Mark laughs. "All right! We were hot!"

"I think we're _____," Robert smiles. "Will, how about you and I go down to the Green Spider and get us a job?"

"No can do," says Will. "Whoever heard of a band with no name?"

"**That** could be our _____: **Band With No Name**."

"How about: Band With No Singer," says Mark. He gives Robert a smile. "Don't take this wrong, Robert—great song. But you do sound like a sick dog."

"And so do you," Jared tells Mark.

"And so do you," Mark tells Jared.

"And so do I," Will tells them all.

Robert says, "I _____ that makes all of us."

"I have an idea for a name," says Jared. "How about **The Sick Dogs**? Every band needs some little thing to set it _____. Our thing could be that we can't sing."

"Oh, that should pull people in," says Robert.

Will sets his guitar down and sits back. "You know that is our big problem. We need a singer. Me—I need a new guitar. This old thing has a crack in it."

114

Name: _____ Date: _____

"I know where you can _____ up a new guitar for next to nothing," says Robert. "A guy tried to sell one to me the other day. I turned him down. This is where you can reach him, if you're interested." Robert hands over a paper on which he has written: 555–7670.

Will takes the paper, then shakes his head. "I'm not buying a _____ guitar."

"How about buying a new one?" asks Robert. "Don't you have a job now?"

"Yes, but I have to save my _____. I need a car even more than a new guitar," says Will.

Jared says, "How are we going to play at the Green Spider if you don't get a new guitar?"

All the boys laugh. "I don't know," says Will. "I guess the world _____ going to hear from The Sick Dogs anytime soon.

115

Name: _____ Date: _____

B. Write the word or words on the line that will correctly complete each sentence.

1. | have just met each other
   | are friends
   | do not get along with each other

   You can tell that the boys _____.

2. | at a baseball game
   | at a school social
   | for people they already know

   Up to now, the band has just been playing music _____

   _____.

3. | are all good singers
   | aren't good enough to play for people they don't know
   | should just joke around and never play music

   The guys in the band think that they _____

   _____.

4. | makes him think of Ana
   | no one seems to like
   | makes him feel happy

   Will is playing a song that _____.

5. | he and the band are going to a city far away to play
   | he is playing well and is really into the music
   | he is going to play with another band

   When Will starts to play, it seems like he is flying. This must mean

   that _____.

116

Name: _____ Date: _____

6. | ready to play for people they don't know
   | not really as good as they thought they should be
   | getting a job at the Green Spider

When Will's song is over, it seems the band thinks that they are _____

_____.

7. | they have all just gotten over having a cold
   | it would be a name that people would like
   | he thinks they sound like sick dogs when they sing

Jared thinks they should call the band **The Sick Dogs** because _____

_____.

8. | a new guitar because his old one has a crack in it
   | another song to sing because one song isn't enough
   | to buy a guitar from the man Robert knows because it is stolen

Will needs _____.

9. | he has a job now
   | he wants to buy a really good guitar
   | he needs to buy a car

Will is saving money because _____.

10. | are sure they will become well-known
    | believe they need Will with them to play at the Green Spider
    | can never play at the Green Spider

From what you have read, you can tell that the guys _____

_____.

Name: _____ Date: _____

C. Write three sentences telling what you would do if you were in the band and might play at the Green Spider.

1. _____
_____
_____

2. _____
_____
_____

3. _____
_____
_____

D. Write three sentences that tell how you think Will feels about music.

1. _____
_____
_____

2. _____
_____
_____

3. _____
_____
_____

Name: _____ Date: _____

MIDWAY ASSESSMENT LEVEL 7

A. Use the words in the box to fill in the blanks. Use each word one time.

across	famous	middle	newspaper	sunny
almost	inside	monster	north	swimming
around	flying	move	shark	window
enough	map	news	someone	winter

It is the coldest day of the winter as two girls, Ana Banks and Robin Hamer, make their way _____ the school grounds to the main door.

"I really think it's g-g-great of you to show me _____ like this," Ana tells Robin as the wind tries its best to drive away her words. She almost has to scream to be heard. "It's hard enough to go to a n-new school in the _____ of the year. I'm so glad I don't have to f-f-find my way around here alone."

"No problem," Robin says, pulling her hat as far down on her head as it will go. "I was new once, so I know w-what it's like."

"Are we _____ there?" asks Ana, feeling frozen from head to foot.

"It's just around this c-c-corner," says Robin, whose hands are like ice and whose eyes are red from the strong wind. The main door cannot open fast _____ for the two girls. They race inside, heading down the hallway.

"Now, **that** feels good!" cries Ana, happy to be _____. "This place is like G-Greenland!" she laughs, still shaking from the snow and wind. "Is it always so cold here in the winter?"

Name: _____ Date: _____

Robin laughs too. "Have you looked at a _____?" she jokes. "We **are** pretty far north! But the answer to your question is no. This is a big cold front, even for us."

"Well, that's good _____, anyway," says Ana. "I'm not sure I could take too many days like this one!"

"Where did you _____ from?" asks Robin, sitting down.

"Believe it or not," says Ana, "Arizona! Land of hot, _____ days and, well—hot, dark nights! Talk about going from one pole to the other!"

"I'll say!" says Robin. "What made you move so far _____?"

"My dad took over the family business from my grandma last summer," says Ana. "He was _____ back on weekends while Mom and I tried to sell the house. We did that a week ago, so here I am!"

"I think you'll like Henson High School," says Robin. "Most of the kids are great. Maybe I can introduce you to _____ who likes the same kinds of things as you. What did you like to do in Arizona?"

"I was on the swim team," Ana laughs, "for all the good it will do me here!" She looks out the picture _____ into the driving snow and laughs again. "I guess I should have put a little more time into _____ sports."

120

"Was there anything else?" asks Robin, sitting back and putting her feet up.

"Yes," says Ana, "when I wasn't _____, I was working on our school newspaper, *The Short Cut.* I want to become a _____ writer for one of the big papers someday. My dad says Henson High has a _____, too, so I should feel right at home."

"Only if you're used to living with a _____," Robin says with a smile, shaking her head.

"What do you mean?" Ana wants to know.

"Just look at it this way," says Robin, "if Henson High were the open sea, then Jared Stormer would be the _____ you have to watch out for!"

121

Name: _____ Date: _____

B. Write the phrase on the line that will correctly complete each sentence.

1. | they both know what it's like to be cold
   | they both know what it's like to be new
   | they don't have any other friends but each other

   Ana seems to get along with Robin because _____
   _____.

2. | she has moved to Greenland
   | she has moved to Arizona
   | she has moved far north, and it's winter

   Ana feels cold because _____.

3. | Ana is used to living in Arizona where it's not cold
   | Robin has never been to Arizona
   | Ana doesn't have a hat to wear

   Ana seems to feel the cold more than Robin. Maybe that's because
   _____.

4. | played on the baseball team
   | was on the swim team
   | hated to play basketball

   In Arizona, Ana _____.

5. | her dad and her mom had been fighting, and they didn't all want to be together that much
   | her dad took over the family business from Grandma, and he didn't have time to see Ana and her mom
   | her dad's work was up north, and Ana and her mom were trying to sell the house in Arizona

   Ana's dad had only been with Ana and her mom on weekends because
   _____
   _____.

122

Name: _____ Date: _____

6. | he knows about the school newspaper
   | he went to Henson High School when he lived there
   | Grandma told him a lot

   You can tell that Ana's dad has learned something about Henson High

   School because _____

   _____.

7. | swimming and winter sports
   | the school newspaper and swimming
   | making friends and working on the school newspaper

   The two most important things for Ana at her old school were

   _____

   _____.

8. | a good friend to Robin
   | someone who doesn't like Ana at all
   | someone who Ana will need to watch carefully

   It seems that Jared Stormer is _____

   _____.

9. | cause a lot of problems at school because she's new
   | stand up to other people and fight with them
   | like to make friends with others

   Ana seems like the kind of person who would _____

   _____.

10. | there will be a big fight at school
    | Ana and Jared will have problems
    | Ana and Robin will have problems

    From what you have read, you can guess that _____

    _____.

123

Name: _____ Date: _____

C. Write three sentences telling what you would do if you were Ana and had just moved to a new school.

1. _____
_____
_____

2. _____
_____
_____

3. _____
_____
_____

D. Write three sentences telling how you think Ana should act around Jared.

1. _____
_____
_____

2. _____
_____
_____

3. _____
_____
_____

Name: _____ Date: _____

FINAL ASSESSMENT LEVEL 7

A. Use the words in the box to fill in the blanks. Use each word one time.

ads	couldn't	game	power	always
enough	minutes	sick	basket	famous
money	sometimes	bench	feel	never
special	city	friends	owned	throw

"Stop them!"

The crowd is screaming with excitement. This is not just any basketball game. This is the Cougars against the Sharks. But the _____ is not going well. The Cougars are behind by 10 points.

Spider can't do anything to help. He is sitting on the _____ where he always sits. Out of 12 guys on the team, he is number 12. Two years ago, he wasn't even on the team. He was not very big back then. No one called him Spider. He was Tom to his _____ and "Hey, you" to everyone else. In school, he did just well enough to get by. In his classes, he never talked much. He was OK at playground games, but not great. There was just nothing _____ about him.

Back then, the game he played most was baseball. His best friend, Mark, was pretty good at it. He played in the park and _____ Tom went along. Mark always made sure Tom was picked for a team. Tom was not a bad player. He was fast. He could field pretty well. He just _____ hit. Mark would tell him, "Hey, some guys have it, and some guys don't." Tom would laugh—he didn't mind the joke.

125

Name: _____   Date: _____

Tom had been living with his aunt and uncle ever since his parents died. Uncle Robert _____ a car shop. He did body work on cars. He had two guys working for him. When Tom and Mark became 14, Uncle Robert put them both to work. At first he just had them help the older guys. But as time went by, he gave them chances to learn the business. As they learned, he gave them more to do—and more _____, too.

Then Tom started to grow—and grow. He went from 5'4" to 6'3" in one year. His arms and legs became so long, he could hardly tell what they were doing anymore. His legs were _____ getting caught in things. His feet were just too far away to know what his head wanted. His hands had minds of their own. He could hardly make it across a room without falling over.

One day in the park, someone said to him, "Hey, Spider! _____ me the ball." No one had called him Spider before that day. After that day, everyone called him Spider. A name like that can stick for life. Tom had been Spider ever since that day.

Toward the end of that year, Spider was big _____ to be in the basketball games on the other side of the park. Now Mark came with him sometimes. Spider always made sure Mark was picked. Spider was not that good at the game himself at first. But he could fill a lot of space under the _____.

His friends said he should try out for the high school basketball team. JFK High School had one of the best teams in the _____. They even went to the state championship once. They didn't win, but you can't have everything. That team is still _____ around the school. A picture of that team is still hanging in the office. But the boys from that team were all men now.

126

One of them now sells used cars in town. You can see his
_____ on late night TV. "Come on down!" he would
scream. "Let Mad Mack fix you up!" Another player is now in politics.

Spider made the team when he was 16. He was happy just to
be put on the team. He _____ started a game. In fact,
he hardly ever played in a real game that year. But he thought
the practice games were fun.

Now, however, Spider is in his last year of high school. He is
growing into his body. His arms and legs _____ like his
own. He knows he is playing much better on the playground.
He's no longer happy just to sit on the bench. He wants to be in
some real games. The trouble is he plays power forward, and the
team already has a star _____ forward. Tyrone is his
name. He has been starting for three years. People say he **owns**
the team. They say he is going to make a big name for himself in
college ball. His name is in the paper sometimes. The team even
has a good player to back him up. When Tyrone needs a rest, this
other guy goes in for a few _____. Coach Pack never
keeps Tyrone out for much longer than that. So Spider never has
his turn on the floor.

Tonight will be different. Spider is excited. He knows he is
going to be in the game tonight. The other forward is out
_____. When Tyrone needs a break, the coach will have
to put Spider in the game. Spider keeps a close eye on the game,
trying to get a feel for it. He wants to be ready.

Name: _____   Date: _____

B. Write the word or words on the line that will correctly complete each sentence.

1. | was on the playground a lot and good at sports
    | was quiet and not into sports
    | was good at sports but didn't like to play

    You get the idea that when Spider was younger, he _____

    _____ .

2. | his parents died
    | he liked his aunt and uncle
    | his aunt and uncle let him do what he wanted

    Tom lived with his aunt and uncle because _____ .

3. | worked all of the time
    | helped older guys and made a lot of money
    | learned the business and started to make more money

    Uncle Robert gave Tom and Mark jobs, and they _____

    _____ .

4. | his parents didn't know him
    | he couldn't hit the ball in the park anymore
    | he was having trouble making his arms and legs do what he wanted them to do

    When Tom started to grow, he grew so fast that _____

    _____ .

5. | by Mark
    | by his parents
    | by someone in the park

    Spider is the name that Tom was given _____ .

Name: _____ Date: _____

6. | be in the basketball games in the park
   | lead the team at JFK High School to a big win
   | work for Mad Mack

After Spider had gotten bigger, it seems he was ready to _____

_____.

7. | he was still learning the game and needed more practice
   | he didn't like to play in the real games, only in the practice games
   | the coach thought he was just not big enough yet

When Spider first got on the high school team, he didn't play in the real

games much because _____.

8. | he thinks his name—not Tyrone's—should be in the paper
   | he knows he's a better player than Tyrone
   | he wasn't happy sitting on the bench all the time

Now that Spider is in his last year of high school, he wants to be in some

real games because _____.

9. | Coach Pack told him he would play
   | Tyrone's backup is sick and Tyrone will need a rest
   | he is the only forward that the team has left

Spider **knows** that he'll get a chance to play tonight because _____

_____.

10. | works hard, studies the game, and wants to do his best
    | wants to make a big name for himself in college ball
    | will do anything he can to take Tyrone's place on the team

From what you have read, you can tell that Spider is the kind of person who

_____.

129

Administering the High Frequency Words Quizzes

The purpose of the High Frequency Words Quizzes is to assess students' recognition and comprehension of high frequency words. The quizzes include many of the words students encounter while using the *Caught Reading* program. Therefore, students should display a mastery of most of these words based on their exposure to them. However, students who are still having reading difficulties in the secondary grades may not have mastered all the words on these lists.

Often, students know a word, but do not recognize it, and the lack of recognition hinders their reading. Administering the High Frequency Words Quizzes can provide the essential foundation to build and assess fluency and automaticity. The administration procedure asks the teacher to say the word, read a sentence that uses the word in context, and then repeat the word. By reading the word in context, students are tasked with (1) comprehending the word within a specific context and (2) demonstrating their recognition of that word by spelling it. For example, if the high frequency word is "to," students would have to demonstrate the ability to differentiate "to" from its homophones "two" and "too." Then, they spell the correct version of the word, attesting to their recognition of the correct form.

Directions

1. Before administering the High Frequency Words Quizzes…
- Make one copy for each student of the appropriate High Frequency Words Quizzes located on pages 131–137 of this *Manual*.
- Make one copy of the High Frequency Words Mastery Chart located on page 192 of this *Manual*. Students record the scores on the quizzes on this chart.

2. Administer the High Frequency Words Quizzes.
Time: 20 minutes (per quiz)
- Ask students to number their papers for the amount of words in the list.
- Remind students that these are the words they must have 100 percent correct in order to move on to the next Level in *Caught Reading*.
- Read the first word, being careful to pronounce it correctly. Then, use it in a sentence that demonstrates its meaning. Finally, repeat the word again. Repeat the process for each word. Move quickly through the list, as these words should be spelled automatically. If students cannot spell the words quickly, they do not know them well enough.

3. Score the High Frequency Words Quizzes.
- When you finish the quiz, help students to correct their papers.
- Students record their scores on the High Frequency Words Mastery Chart on page 192 of this *Manual*.
- Students write any words not spelled correctly on the bottom of the High Frequency Words Mastery Chart. Students study this list of words until mastery is achieved in a quick and automatic manner.
- Students can quiz each other, using only the words they missed on the quiz. Remind students that when quizzing each other, they should move through the list quickly, giving their partner only a few seconds to write down the word.
- After mastery of a word has been achieved, that word should then be spelled correctly in all written work.
- When all spelling tests for a Level are completed, students who have not yet achieved 100 percent mastery should continue to practice toward that goal. Movement to the next Level should not take place until that goal has been achieved.

The high frequency words for each Level are selected from the:

(1) *Caught Reading* Word List for that Level (excluding proper nouns, selection-specific words not considered to be high frequency, and words repeated from a prior Level);

(2) words that are not in *Caught Reading* but are listed in the Dolch List (Grades Preprimer–3) and Fry's Essential Words (first 600 words—Grades 1–4).

High Frequency Words Quiz: Level 1

Level 1 List 1 (26 words)	Level 1 List 2 (25 words)	Level 1 List 3 (25 words)	Level 1 List 4 (25 words)	Level 1 List 5 (25 words)	Level 1 List 6 (25 words)	Level 1 List 7 (25 words)
little	making	off	house	bags	girls	was
doing	team	try	say	faster	new	college
kids	bikes	careful	wood	lot	to	hit
she	for	he	dad	takes	calls	problems
thinking	man	on	if	be	going	we
don't	teamwork	trying	says	fastest	next	come
laugh	boss	hear	woods	lots	can	hitting
sick	friend	one	is	talk	grandma	put
about	me	us	scared	big	night	week
laughing	that	help	work	find	can't	comes
sister	boy	own	it	make	hall	home
ad	friends	waiting	school	talking	not	race
drink	mom	class	working	bigger	truck	what
laughs	the	helped	day	finds	cannot	coming
sleep	boyfriend	part	scream	makes	happy	hot
am	game	walk	you	talks	of	Saturday
drinker	money	classes	did	bike	trucks	who
light	then	helps	screams	fire	car	cook
sleeping	bus	people	your	dogs	wants	girl
are	get	walks	do	kid	coach	need
drive	more	clean	job	selling	his	time
like	think	her	see	have	problem	call
sorry	but	play	does	back	sell	by
back	gets	want	sees	fast	player	stop
drives	my	cleaning	dog	lost	take	keep
hide						

131

High Frequency Words Quiz: Level 2

Level 2 List 1 (23 words)	Level 2 List 2 (23 words)	Level 2 List 3 (23 words)	Level 2 List 4 (23 words)	Level 2 List 5 (23 words)	Level 2 List 6 (22 words)	Level 2 List 7 (23 words)
alive	at	throws	idea	lighten	snowball	present
feels	old	because	wall	shop	snowing	ran
maybe	there	having	it's	will	worth	seem
after	away	principal	says	line	ever	shall
field	getting	up	wanted	should	mad	tree
meet	other	believe	close	window	sold	until
sun	they	him	screaming	dark	some	morning
all	give	raise	cold	lines	feel	mother
fires	our	use	wave	sleeping	may	near
most	bad	raised	just	woman	start	only
taken	gives	uses	sea	days	upon	looking
already	over	biggest	waves	long	wish	snow
fish	thinks	hold	kidding	smash	three	worked
Mrs.	band	raises	seen	won	which	looks
talking	pack	vote	way	didn't	also	when
another	this	boat	cop	longer	best	laughs
fished	bank	holds	wear	smashed	came	ship
anymore	three	votes	know	dinner	dear	I'll
friendly	base	homeless	wearing	look	end	running
needed	hard	run	knows	smashing	four	walking
tell	paint	walked	shelter	doesn't	left	champion
apartment	throw	has	no	tells	painter	baseball
gave						

High Frequency Words Quiz: Level 3

Level 3 List 1 (25 words)	Level 3 List 2 (24 words)	Level 3 List 3 (25 words)	Level 3 List 4 (25 words)	Level 3 List 5 (25 words)	Level 3 List 6 (24 words)	Level 3 List 7 (24 words)
again	somewhere	outside	things	introduction	even	words
games	bases	box	cards	room	leave	far
move	got	happens	homework	took	saw	likes
smile	sound	owns	points	runs	were	she's
always	been	than	pretty	tries	every	works
much	group	boxes	through	sad	leaves	feelings
smiles	oh	paints	houses	turn	what's	looked
anything	sounds	that's	pull	dog's	everyone	shops
must	before	buy	till	keeps	let	would
so	guy	he's	change	safe	while	write
anyway	starts	place	pulls	turns	everything	show
myself	behind	their	today	said	let's	wrong
someday	had	called	circle	under	why	first
as	open	hears	puts	done	everywhere	showing
name	believes	places	together	kitchen	lets	yes
somehow	hand	them	read	sale	self	food
asks	opens	here	told	door	without	made
needs	story	players	inside	sales	face	shows
someone	below	these	reads	down	letter	you're
attach	happen	himself	could	last	sells	forget
gone	or	playing	into	same	word	side
news	better	thing	right	else	fame	yourself
something	mind	card	too	save	lights	mean
from	happened	sit	mouth	sits	sentence	sisters
now		point	cries	well		

133

High Frequency Words Quiz: Level 4

Level 4 List 1 (25 words)	Level 4 List 2 (24 words)	Level 4 List 3 (25 words)	Level 4 List 4 (25 words)	Level 4 List 5 (24 words)	Level 4 List 6 (24 words)	Level 4 List 7 (24 words)
against	animals	ball	live	ground	win	darkest
direction	pointed	leave	saved	shake	course	hope
spiders	sticks	red	trap	voices	helping	creatures
air	answers	teeth	cage	grow	shakes	parts
in	enough	feelers	front	hands	never	space
stand	keep	ants	trip	lives	sky	die
drug	push	remembers	balls	metal	crack	helpless
insect	still	they're	gang	shark	oil	houses
planet	planets	belongs	living	water	ones	harmful
star	ant	radios	gas	computer	small	pay
always	eye	legs	cars	monster	sharks	cracks
each	pushed	fight	changed	ways	crash	different
insects	stops	robot	lose	harm	hiding	pictures
jobs	kind	between	eyes	fights	harmed	spider
stars	stories	life	used	mountains	solid	best
and	arm	pushes	changes	sickness	year	draw
earth	fall	those	fighting	weeks	creature	eight
plant	questions	kinds	given	corner	hits	only
starts	studies	body	seem	using	outer	seven
animal	attacks	fix	rock	moves	yet	years
eat	falls	times	circles	count	cut	six
interested	known	break	glass	harmless	hole	warm
plants	radio	fly	machine	names	page	you'll
steal	land	liquid	green	seems	sometimes	sitting
eats		toward	voice			

High Frequency Words Quiz: Level 5

Level 5 List 1 (23 words)	Level 5 List 2 (23 words)	Level 5 List 3 (22 words)	Level 5 List 4 (22 words)	Level 5 List 5 (22 words)	Level 5 List 6 (22 words)	Level 5 List 7 (22 words)
accident	asking	born	two	counts	hour	around
fair	law	tried	mine	holding	owned	ate
husband	pulled	build	handouts	miners	stopped	bed
paying	tent	union	share	neighborhood	yellow	highest
stronger	badly	finish	building	south	however	dress
act	laws	burns	hanged	crops	neighbors	miles
families	beat	California	went	days	pants	happy
jean	five	tents	chief	homes	strike	along
pick	learn	gold	harder	office	hurt	workers
strongly	putting	jeans	white	started	starting	blanket
pickers	test	good	cleaned	worker	passed	lived
swim	become	voting	named	camps	strong	town
farm	found	camp	shoe	days	driver	stayed
joke	thief	grape	closed	hood	o'clock	eating
pipe	becoming	farming	heads	drive	carry	hoped
Americans	free	married	nation	hope	wagons	lasted
farmers	believed	wagon	willing	opened	coat	poor
kill	freeway	meeting	cloth	stay	fine	asked
police	reading	growers	high	others	funny	late
fields	bill	mile	navy	writing	hopes	finding
sending	listened	screams	social	growing	neighbor	stood
guys	ready	waited	wins	dying	winter	years
history	cares					

High Frequency Words Quiz: Level 6

Level 6 List 1 (29 words)	Level 6 List 2 (29 words)	Level 6 List 3 (29 words)	Level 6 List 4 (29 words)	Level 6 List 5 (29 words)	Level 6 List 6 (29 words)	Level 6 List 7 (28 words)
across	she'll	bones	knees	freeze	suddenly	handle
driving	anyone	isn't	paper	liked	couldn't	telling
hearing	Mr.	north	soon	plays	glasses	dishes
rocks	apartments	washing	web	stolen	wouldn't	hands
adventures	hiding	books	feet	won't	country	rhymes
early	music	fallen	park	charts	pushing	means
heat	shut	nothing	bursts	freezing	sure	rich
men	very	wasn't	fell	liking	great	doors
top	arms	both	lands	poems	reach	hat
alone	since	falling	few	coldest	love	meat
helper	excited	turning	stairs	frozen	you've	ride
might	sing	older	excitement	storm	main	medal
trips	banks	watch	whatever	full	excites	money
eaten	singing	boys	camping	pole	young	order
trouble	needs	fancy	standing	street	rent	round
either	explore	sometime	sings	cool	dirt	sat
turned	sled	we'll	whole	explorers	gun	ten
electric	beginning	breaking	slow	lock	rest	set
hero	electricity	fat	floor	prove	telephone	though
moved	noise	we're	placing	such	dirty	six
secret	slowly	feeling	follow	longest	guys	third
hey	war	packing	letters	sudden	restaurant	return
grade	guess	hair	hill	thank	seven	summer
lady	note	plan	quite	reason	remain	teacher
milk	past	road	service	several	short	bread
egg	cry	cow	cost	class	bridge	wind
bird	begin	age	add	yard	world	sent
sir	spell	spring	train	son	speak	children
moving	wash	song	windows	world	dish	

High Frequency Words Quiz: Level 7

Level 7 List 1 (32 words)	Level 7 List 2 (32 words)	Level 7 List 3 (32 words)	Level 7 List 4 (32 words)	Level 7 List 5 (32 words)	Level 7 List 6 (32 words)	Level 7 List 7 (32 words)
above	article	doctor	brother	carefully	moment	toward
correctly	important	bench	faces	forgets	month	hear
numbers	paragraph	engine	facts	low	winning	appear
slams	information	jumps	quick	form	clock	rather
ads	parents	playground	business	catch	grouped	visit
court	stands	black	list	uncle	shop	began
hides	passes	suppose	rooms	forward	closely	airplane
once	aunt	keeping	tomorrow	score	movie	twelve
ago	dream	block	fill	supposed	clothes	whether
crowd	interesting	example	listed	center	hair	supply
hour	person	power	rule	mark	company	being
almost	state	table	tonight	understand	hangs	city
others	basket	practice	buys	second	filling	thought
answers	drivers	taking	listening	fun	sign	became
darker	stays	breath	rules	chance	newspaper	evening
pages	basketball	exciting	following	minute	skill	public
special	easy	price	tool	choice	yesterday	feed
pair	piece	teams	calm	missing	heading	correct
huts	step	bring	foods	sells	number	during
directions	baskets	learning	foot	giving	slam	father
ideas	empty	problems	loud	model	younger	large
papers	pieces	less	sales	shoot	matter	late
twenty	whose	wife	wonder	wrote	real	result
rode	serve	sort	whom	women	system	themselves
river	thousand	thus	herself	human	increase	itself
baby	case	cause	condition	consider	continue	demand
drop	eleven	fear	felt	figure	force	fourth
glad	flew	church	charge	chair	certain	beautiful
among	afternoon	able	tried	suit	shoes	party
miss	hundred	held	half	government	garden	cover
kept	king	knew	labor	least	lie	national
sport	store	pulling	trick	clap	lost	receive

POSTASSESSMENT

The Postassessment stage is designed to ensure student mastery of skills and concepts presented in *Caught Reading*. Once students pass the Posttests, they are ready to proceed to a reading strategies program such as *Be A Better Reader*.

The Posttests are designed to verify that students have mastered the *Caught Reading* program. The Posttests can be found on pages 140–143 of this *Manual*. These tests are administered to the whole class. Students read the passages silently and respond to comprehension questions as directed. Both Posttests are at the same reading Level. The difference is that Posttest A is an expository passage, while Posttest B is a narrative passage. The posttests cannot be used interchangeably and both should be administered. The postassessment passages can provide a final evaluation of students' accomplishments in *Caught Reading*, as well as determine their readiness for other curriculum materials. Postassessment should be administered only after students have completed Level 7 of *Caught Reading*. Following are two options for evaluating your students' progress:

OPTION 1
- Administer Posttest A and Posttest B. (See Directions section below.)
- Students who score an average of 90-100 percent on both Posttests should be placed in *Be a Better Reader: Level A*.
- Students who score an average of 85 percent or less on both Posttests should be placed in *Be a Better Reader: Starting Out*.
- Students who score an average of 50 percent or less on both Posttests may require reteaching. Therefore, begin by examining the work they completed for *Caught Reading*.

OPTION 2
- In lieu of administering the Posttests, you can base your assessment on the grades students received for the work they did for *Caught Reading*.
- Students who averaged grades in the "A" range for all levels of *Caught Reading* and seemed bored with the material can be placed in *Be A Better Reader: Level A*.
- Students who averaged grades in the "B" range for all levels of *Caught Reading* can be placed in *Be A Better Reader: Starting Out*.
- Students who averaged grades in the "C" range for all levels of *Caught Reading* may be ready for *Be A Better Reader: Starting Out*.
- Students who averaged grades in the "D" or "F" range for all levels of *Caught Reading* may require reteaching. Therefore, begin by examining the work they completed for *Caught Reading*.

Directions

1. Before administering the Posttests...
- Make one copy for each student of Posttest A or B Passage located on pages 140 and 142 of this *Manual*.
- Make one copy for each student of Posttest A or B Comprehension Questions located on pages 141 and 143 of this *Manual*. Students will record their answers on these sheets.

2. Administer the Posttests.

Time: One class period per Posttest (approximately 45 minutes)

- Tell students to take this process seriously and to do their best. Tell them that the information gained from the Initial Filter will help plan their instructional program.
- Explain to students that they may read the passage as many times as needed to become familiar with it.
- Remind students that when they finish reading the passage you will be collecting it. Tell them that they will not have the passage when they are answering the comprehension questions.
- Tell students that they do not have to answer the open-ended questions in complete sentences and that spelling errors will not lower their grade. However, encourage students to do their best in those areas, as well as write neatly, so their answers can easily be read.
- Tell students that they should keep the answers to the open-ended items (Questions 7–10) brief but complete and based on what they read in the text.
- Explain to students that there are no time limits for reading the passage or answering the questions.
- Tell students that the answers to some of the questions may not be directly stated in the passage.
- Distribute copies of the Posttest A Passage. Read the directions with students, and have them begin the passage.
- Collect Posttest A Passage from each student as they finish reading, and distribute Posttest A Comprehension Questions.
- Repeat the last two steps for Posttest B.

3. Score the Posttests and interpret the results.

- Use the Posttest answer keys on pages 144–145 of this *Manual* to assess the number of correct answers. Then, review the guidelines under Option 1 on page 138 of this *Manual* to determine the next steps for each student.
- Questions 1–5 are recall questions.
- Question 6 is a vocabulary question.
- Question 7 is a summarization question.
- Questions 8 and 9 are inferential questions.
- Question 10 is an evaluation question.
- For inferential questions 8–9 and evaluative question 10, students' responses must relate to the information in the passage and must add ideas and information from their own thoughts, supported by appropriate reasoning. To be completely correct, the answer must include a response to the "Explain your answer" portion of the question. Half credit may be given for an answer that gives a good response to the first part, but does not explain why the response was given.
- For the vocabulary question, the definition cannot include the target word. If it is not one of the choices given in the answer key, it must reflect the meaning of the word as used in the passage.

POSTTEST A: Passage

Directions: Read the passage below. You may read it as many times as you need to for complete understanding. When you are finished, raise your hand, and the teacher will bring you a set of questions to answer. Remember, you will not have the passage when answering the questions.

A balloon is known as a "lighter-than-air craft." How can this be? We know that air is lighter than almost anything. A balloon can't really be "lighter" than air. So what keeps it up?

Every material has a certain density, or thickness of matter. Air is not very dense. Rocks and steel are quite dense.

If you heat up air, it becomes less dense. The molecules move around a lot more when the air is hot. The moving molecules take up more space. If you fill a balloon with hot air, the air in the balloon is less dense than the air outside the balloon. That denser air around the balloon pushes in against the balloon and forces it upward. If the upward force is more than the weight of the balloon and the air inside it, the balloon will float upward.

A hot-air balloon has several parts. The bag is made of strong cloth-like nylon. The cloth is covered with rubber to keep it from leaking. A net of ropes on the outside of the bag helps to keep the balloon's shape and supports the basket, or gondola, below. The bottom of the balloon is called the neck. Hanging inside the neck is a propane burner for heating the air.

A balloonist makes the balloon rise by heating the air at the neck. The hot air is less dense and rises into the bag. As hot air enters the bag, the colder air inside is forced out of the neck. When the bag has expanded enough, it begins to float. Soon, the balloon, with its burner, basket, and passengers, rises into the air. The balloonist can then shut off the burner.

As the air in the balloon begins to cool, the air in it takes up less space. The air around the balloon has less to push on, so the balloon begins to come down. The balloonist can control the rising and sinking of the balloon very precisely by running the burner and shutting it off. Short bursts of hot air can keep the balloon at one level. Longer bursts can make it rise.

POSTTEST A: Comprehension Questions

Directions: Please respond to each question in writing. There is no time limit. Spelling and punctuation will not be graded, but you should do your best.

1. What happens if you heat air? _____

2. Name at least two parts of a hot-air balloon. _____

3. What is used to heat the air inside the balloon? _____

4. How does a balloonist make a balloon rise? _____

5. What kind of bursts of air keep the balloon level? _____

6. Explain what the word *expanded* means in this sentence from the passage: "When the bag has <u>expanded</u> enough, it begins to float."
   _____

7. What is this passage mostly about? _____

8. What are some problems that might make it difficult to steer the balloon?
   _____

9. How do you think the balloonist would get the balloon back down to the ground?
   _____

10. Would you want to ride in a hot-air balloon? Explain your answer.
    _____

POSTTEST B: Passage

Directions: Read the passage below. You may read it as many times as you need to for complete understanding. When you are finished, raise your hand, and the teacher will bring you a set of questions to answer. Remember, you will not have the passage when answering the questions.

Excitement ran through Tom Swift Eagle as he looked out the plane window. This would be his training unit's first jump with other firefighters.

These firefighters belonged to a special group called smoke jumpers. They were trained to jump from planes to fight fires. They jumped in parts of a forest that could not be reached by firefighters on the ground. Tom thought smoke jumpers were the bravest men alive. Today he would have the chance to use all that John Dull Knife had taught him. He would show himself to be as brave as the bravest smoke jumper.

Tom pressed his face to the plane window and watched the green woods below him. Then he saw it. Great clouds of thick, black smoke were foaming up in the sky. His heart beat faster and faster.

It was almost time to jump. Jumping at the right instant was important. Smoke jumpers have to land near the fire without falling into the hungry flames.

At John's signal, Tom leaped out of the plane. He slowly dropped through the smoky air. He dropped down, down, toward the raging fire. He guided his parachute to an open spot between the trees. He had learned how to keep his parachute from getting hung up in tree branches.

As Tom hit the ground, the sharp smell of burning wood surrounded him. He heard the great fire roaring in the distance like a huge waterfall.

The firefighters quickly put on their hard hats and protective gloves. Armed with shovels and axes, they set to work making a firebreak. They cut down trees and cleared away brush on a wide strip of land in front of the racing flames. Then they scraped away some of the soil till bare ground showed. When the fire reached this bare ground, it would have nothing to feed on and would stop.

It would stop if they could finish in time.

Name _____ Date _____

POSTTEST B: Comprehension Questions

Directions: Please respond to each question in writing. There is no time limit. Spelling and punctuation will not be graded, but you should do your best.

1. What were the firefighters trained to do? _____

2. How would Tom show himself to be brave? _____

3. When Tom looked out the plane window, what did he see? _____

4. How did Tom know it was OK to leap from the plane? _____

5. What did the firefighters put on to protect themselves? _____

6. Explain what the word *foaming* means in this sentence from the passage: "Great clouds of thick, black smoke were <u>foaming</u> up in the sky."

7. What is this passage mostly about? _____

8. What kind of training do you think Tom needed for his job?

9. Why do you think Tom thought smoke jumpers were the bravest men alive?

10. Do you think the firefighters were able to finish in time to stop the fire? Explain your answer.

Posttest Answer Key

Posttest A

Recall

1. What happens if you heat air? *It gets less dense; it gets lighter; molecules move around and take up less space.*
2. Name at least two parts of a hot-air balloon. *bag; neck; net of ropes; basket; propane burner*
3. What is used to heat the air inside a balloon? *propane burner*
4. How does a balloonist make the balloon rise? *heats the air at the neck; hot air; hot air forces cold air out*
5. What kind of bursts of air keep the balloon level? *short ones*

Vocabulary

6. Explain what the word *expanded* means in this sentence from the passage: "When the bag has <u>expanded</u> enough, it begins to float." *get bigger; get larger; stretch*

Topic/Title

7. What is this passage mostly about? *hot-air balloons; how hot-air balloons work*

Inference

8. What are some problems that might make it difficult to steer the balloon? *Accept any logical answer: bad weather; too many passengers; people get scared; balloonist gets sick.*
9. How do you think the balloonist would get the balloon back down to the ground? *Accept any logical response related to turning off the burner or letting the air cool completely.*

Evaluation

10. Would you want to ride in a hot-air balloon? Explain your answer. *Accept any logical response supported by appropriate reasoning.*

Posttest Answer Key (Continued)

Posttest B

Recall

1. What were the firefighters trained to do? *jump from planes to fight fires*
2. How would Tom show himself to be brave? *He would use what John Dull Knife had taught him.*
3. When he looked out the plane window, what did Tom see? *thick, black smoke; green woods*
4. How did Tom know it was okay to leap from the plane? *John signaled at the right time.*
5. What did the firefighters put on to protect themselves? *hard hats and protective gloves*

Vocabulary

6. Explain what the word *foaming* means in this sentence from the passage: "Great clouds of thick, black smoke were foaming up in the sky." *bubbling up; going higher and higher; piling up*

Topic/Title

7. What is this passage mostly about? *a smoke jumper; jumping from a plane to fight fires*

Inference

8. What kind of training do you think Tom needed for his job? *Accept any logical response: skydiving; firefighting.*
9. Why do you think Tom thought smoke jumpers were the bravest men alive? *Accept any logical response: They risked their lives; they could be burned to death; they jumped from planes.*

Evaluation

10. Do you think the firefighters were able to finish in time to stop the fire? Explain your answer. *Accept any logical response: They worked hard to prepare the ground; they were trained well; the fire was too hot, and it overcame them.*

READING IN YOUR CLASSROOM

Why Is Reading Assessment Important?

The answer to this question is simple: Assessment informs instruction. Ongoing assessment of students' progress provides specific data that allows teachers to effectively target the needs of their students and students to take charge of their own learning. Planning instruction based on results allows teachers to determine areas needing direct instruction, review, or practice. Informing students of assessment results serves to make them part of the solution and aware of their responsibility in the learning process. Together, teachers and students can create and implement a successful plan that provides for specific instruction and assessment to continually monitor progress and achievement.

Students in middle school believe that they should be able to read and write within the expectations of these grade-level requirements. The frustration displayed is the gap between what the students think they should know and be able to do and what they actually know and are able to do. Instruction designed to address the results of the assessment gives students the chance to start where they are and quickly move forward, sometimes for the first time in their educational experience.

Assessment can take many forms, ranging from mandated standardized testing and informal reading inventories to writing samples, criterion-referenced tests, and teacher observation. It is critical to gather as much data as possible about each student in order to analyze, diagnose, and plan targeted instruction. A typical list might include many of these:

Formal, structured assessment	Informal, less-structured assessment
Informal reading inventories (IRIs)	Portfolios
Norm-referenced tests (NRTs)	Writing samples
Criterion-referenced tests (CRTs)	Student self-assessment
Spelling inventories	Oral reading by students for evaluation purposes
Diagnostic tests	Interviews with students and parents
	Sustained Silent Reading (SSR) records (title, amount/type of books read)
	Journals
	Teacher observation

The information gathered from this assessment may be used for:

Analysis: What did the student do? Why?

Interpretation: What can the student do?

Diagnosis: What support does the student need?

Planning: What strategies and skills does the student need to learn and practice?

Ongoing checks (administered at least on a quarterly basis): How is the student progressing? What is the evidence? What revisions/additions to the plan are needed?

Evaluation: How are the student's skills growing and progressing?

It is important to take the time for assessment. Failure to do so may leave many students and teachers without the necessary information to truly improve and show growth toward meeting expectations.

Have Student Needs Changed?

"Adolescents entering the world in the 21st century will read and write more than at any other time in human history. They will need advanced levels of literacy to perform their jobs, run their households, act as citizens, and conduct their personal lives. They will need literacy to cope with the flood of information they will find everywhere they turn. They will need literacy to feed their imagination, so they can create the world of the future. In a complex and sometimes dangerous world, their ability to read will be crucial" (Moore et al 1999).

When tested with the same instruments used in the 40s and 50s, students' performance is comparable to the students of that era. In today's world, however, students must begin learning at a much earlier age, and the requirements are more extensive. To function in the 21st century, students must be able to read widely for a variety of purposes, both inside and outside the educational setting.

To further complicate the problem, many struggling readers come from homes that do not provide literacy-rich environments. Consequently, they may have missed from 1,500 to 2,000 hours of reading experiences. These experiences include being read to, rereading familiar stories, and gathering basic knowledge about print. Oral language and listening may also be limited or lacking, thereby preventing students from "banking" words for later transfer to print. Such students begin school far behind students who have had thousands of hours of reading experiences and often never catch up. However, with careful, rigorous instruction, they can improve.

In addition, as educators we are preparing all students, not just those in the 75th percentile, for higher education. Today, we educate all students in our schools to meet the same grade-level standards and performance indicators, regardless of their ability level or their language experiences.

Informal Reading Inventories

The Level Tests, which are the main component of the *Caught Reading Assessment Manual*, are modeled on the process commonly used in informal reading inventories (IRIs). IRIs have been part of the assessment picture since the early 1940s, developed from work done by William S. Gray and others in the early 1900s. Emmet Betts is considered to be the originator, although many others, including Silvaroli, Grey, Botel, Cooper, McCracken, and Sucher and Allred (Johns 2005), have developed their own versions.

IRIs are composed of graded word lists and passages from a variety of sources, accompanied by various types of comprehension questions. Errors made during oral reading, along with responses to accompanying questions, determine student comprehension levels, as well as show strengths and weaknesses in word recognition. Results are rated according to a scoring guide and are used to help plan students' instruction.

Typically, IRIs are given individually as follows:

- The student orally reads graded word lists to determine which passage will be used as the starting point for the assessment.

- The student then reads the appropriate passage orally while the teacher records word recognition errors in a predetermined manner.

- The teacher removes the passage from the student's sight and asks a series of questions. The student responds orally while the teacher records the student's answers. Some inventories suggest that teachers ask students to retell what they have read instead of, or in addition to, answering comprehension questions.

- The student continues to read and respond to passages of increasing difficulty in this manner until a frustration level is reached.

Word-recognition errors are analyzed for how students use strategies in context for identification of unknown words. Responses to comprehension questions are scored to determine student comprehension levels. These scores are combined to calculate independent, instructional, and frustration reading levels. Betts's criteria for word recognition and comprehension to determine instructional levels have remained in use over the years. In most published IRIs, these are set at 90–95 percent accuracy in word recognition and a minimum of 70-75 percent accuracy in responding to comprehension questions (Johns 2005).

Levels of Text Difficulty

Betts determined three levels of text difficulty:

- the independent level
- the instructional level
- the frustration level

It is important to note that levels only have meaning relative to a particular student's ability; they are not absolute measures. These levels help teachers select appropriate reading materials for students. Look at the chart on page 150 of this *Manual* for a detailed description of each level.

The *Caught Reading Assessment Manual* will help you find your students' instructional level. It will also give you information about their independent and frustration levels. All of this information is important to expose students to materials they can comprehend, while at the same time helping them to improve their ability to read and understand.

For many students, their content-area textbooks are frustration-level materials. Indeed, academic language presents an entirely new set of challenges for students. Those who may have been comfortable with lower-level narrative materials may have difficulty transitioning to the expository text found in content-area texts. However, with explicit, targeted instruction in word attack, vocabulary development, and comprehension, students can learn how to access those materials as well.

Levels of Text Difficulty

Independent	Instructional	Frustration
decodes with 95-99% accuracy	decodes with 90-95% accuracy	decodes below 90% accuracy
comprehends with 95-99% accuracy	comprehends with at least 75% accuracy	comprehends with less than 75% accuracy
feels reading is effortless	needs to use effective strategies to comprehend	has no strategies to access text
has necessary background information, experiences, and interest	has limited background information, experiences, and interest	has little or no experiences or interest in text
is familiar with style of language and vocabulary	will need some assistance with vocabulary and language	needs to have the material read aloud by another reader/tape
can read without outside assistance	will need some teacher guidance during reading	requires full assistance of teacher, much scaffolding/discussion
enjoys the reading, able to relax and be entertained	needs to take a more active approach to reading	needs to be greatly encouraged and supported

Appropriate Materials for Each Level

Independent Level

This is the appropriate level for supplementary and recreational reading materials. Most materials used during any sustained silent reading program and recreation or extending reading outside of class should be at this level unless student interest or background knowledge motivates them to struggle through more difficult texts. Obviously, this means classroom and school libraries need to be stocked with a wide variety of reading levels and genres, and students need to be guided in selecting what is manageable and appropriate for them to read.

Instructional Level

This is the range at which students can work comfortably with teacher guidance—the place at which they will have the best chance of learning by applying reading strategies. Pearson materials such as *Caught Reading* and *Be A Better Reader* are excellent for meeting students' needs to help them become better readers of text at their instructional level.

Frustration Level

Materials at this level should not be used for independent reading. They are appropriate only in a heavily scaffolded reading setting. However, because much of the material in a student's day is at this level, students require reading strategies to help them access text found in social studies and science textbooks and grade-level literature anthologies. Therefore, the *Caught Reading* program, which begins to transition students to content-area reading about halfway through the series, is an important tool. Each of the upper level *Caught Reading* Worktexts includes a unique content or real-world focus so that students can be exposed to a broader vocabulary, including words with Greek and Latin roots and more complex concepts. Thus, students move from "learning to read" to "reading to learn."

Caught Reading Worktext 4: Science

Caught Reading Worktext 5: Social Studies

Caught Reading Worktext 6: Literature

Caught Reading Worktext 7: Life Skills

Once students have completed the *Caught Reading* program, they may move onto *Be A Better Reader* for more focus on content-area reading skill and strategy instruction.

An Approach to Reading

Most experts agree that the best way to develop specific reading skills, such as vocabulary development, fluency, spelling, and decoding is by broad and frequent exposure to reading. By the same token, students may have difficulty accessing texts without explicit skill instruction. The answer is to provide a program that includes direct skill instruction, as well as daily opportunities for varied reading.

Caught Reading was designed to provide this type of instruction. Students are taught skills explicitly and are also immersed in reading from the very first lesson. Instruction is never far removed from application. Every Worktext lesson includes a high interest, completely decodable story for students to read. Skill-based lessons (every other lesson in the series) provide word attack, spelling, and vocabulary work before the story and comprehension afterward. Free lessons allow students to read a story without having to learn or apply new skills. This gives them the chance to develop their confidence and fluency.

In the Worktexts, students also practice their skills in the Practice Lessons and read more decodable texts in the two novels that accompany every Level. Pearson recommends that teachers build a library of books of various genres, reading levels, and interests so that students may do independent reading. The *Caught Reading Teacher's Manual* recommends many novels from the Pearson catalog to give teachers a starting point.

Assessment and Instruction

Assessment is absolutely critical in a reading program. Teachers cannot afford to let students "fall through the cracks," particularly with regard to reading. Reading is the principle method of accessing information in all content areas. Students who do not master the reading process are doomed to lag behind their classmates in every academic subject. Teachers need the tools to be able to identify reading problems and to address them effectively.

This *Manual* is designed to provide teachers with just that tool. The *Manual* allows teachers to gather enough information to effectively place students in *Caught Reading*, as well as to diagnose their reading ability. Teachers can also assess at three stages: before students begin the program (Preassessment), during instruction (Ongoing Assessment), and after students have completed the program (Postassessment).

Implementation

While instruction in the *Caught Reading* program can be categorized into explicit skill development and reading opportunities, the two are never separated in the program. They support and reinforce each other throughout. The following sections explain the details of both categories.

Skill Development

The scope and sequence of the *Caught Reading* program is built around the following key skills necessary for a reading program.

Early literacy skills
(found in the *Getting Ready* component)
1. phonemic awareness
2. alphabetic principle
3. basic phonics skills

Word attack
1. phonetic analysis/synthesis
2. structural analysis/synthesis
   a. inflections
   b. derivations
   c. compounds
3. contextual analysis

Spelling

Vocabulary development

Fluency
1. reading rate
2. word recognition

Comprehension
1. literal
2. inferential
3. critical

Of course, reading skills cannot be learned in isolation. They will have little meaning for students unless they are effectively integrated with the other language arts skills: writing, speaking, and listening. To that end, the *Caught Reading* program has numerous opportunities in every lesson for students to practice and develop their abilities with these skills.

More details about Word Attack, Spelling, Vocabulary Development, Fluency, and Comprehension can be found on pages 162–181 of this *Manual*.

Skill Development Across Levels of *Caught Reading*

ITEM	Level 1	Level 2	Level 3	Level 4	Level 5	Level 6	Level 7
STRUCTURAL ANALYSIS (SPELLING STAGE IN PARENTHESES)							
compound	x	x	x	x	x	x	x
contraction	x	x	x		x	x	x
d (S/A)	x				x		
ed (S/A)	x	x		x	x	x	x
er (S/A)	x	x	x	x	x	x	x
es (S/A)	x	x	x	x	x		
est (S/A)	x	x		x		x	
ing (S/A)	x	x	x	x	x	x	x
s (S/A)	x	x	x	x	x	x	x
's	x		x	x	x	x	x
th (S/A)	x						
en (S/A)		x				x	
less (S/A)		x		x			
ly (S/A)		x		x	x	x	x
n (S/A)		x		x	x		
ful (S/A)				x			
ness (S/A)				x			
y (S/A)					x	x	
ity (S/A)						x	
ment (S/A)						x	
ous (S/A)						x	
SPELLING (SPELLING STAGE IN PARENTHESES)							
drop e-add ing (S/A)	x	x		x	x	x	
word shapes	x	x					
double final cons., add ing (S/A)		x			x	x	x
add d, not ed (S/A)		x			x		
see/seen (S/A)		x			x		
2 vowels, 1st long (W/A)		x		x			
add er, no extra e (S/A)		x					
double final consonant (S/A)		x					
y to i, add es (S/A)		x	x				
es after x (S/A)			x	x	x		

S/A: Structural Analysis
W/A: Word Attack

Skill Development Across Levels of *Caught Reading*

ITEM	Level 1	Level 2	Level 3	Level 4	Level 5	Level 6	Level 7
SPELLING (SPELLING STAGE IN PARENTHESES) *CONTINUED*							
fine e silent, previous vowel long (W/A)			x		x		
vowel sounds ea/ee (W/A)				x			
plural/possessive				x			
y to i, add ly (S/A)					x		
add y, double final consonant (S/A)					x		
i to y, drop e, add ing (S/A)					x		
one vowel, try silent sound (W/A)					x		
drop e, double t, add en (S/A)						x	
COMPREHENSION							
details	x	x	x	x	x	x	x
main idea	x	x	x		x	x	x
ordering ideas	x	x	x	x			
What Do You Think?	x	x			x		x
read again	x		x	x		x	
predictions		x	x		x	x	x
you make the call (inference)			x				
describe it			x		x		
summary/expository				x	x		
then find facts				x			
compare/contrast					x		x
follow the plot						x	
What's the problem? (inference)						x	
sequencing						x	
finding facts to back up main idea						x	
getting to know characters							x
Who's changed? (inference)							x
plot summary (narrative)							x

The Reading Program

A reading program should provide many opportunities for learning at students' instructional and independent reading levels, as well as strategies and approaches for accessing material at their frustration level. For struggling readers in secondary school, academic texts are often at frustration level.

At-risk readers need access to academic texts to keep up with the content demands of their classes, as well as instructional level materials to build strategies that can be applied to grade-level concepts.

Caught Reading recognizes students' needs in "learning to read," but quickly begins the transition to "reading to learn" in the upper-level worktexts. Levels 1–3 contain only narrative text. Levels 4–7 each concentrate on a content area and begin to expose students to expository and real-world texts.

Modes of Reading

Good instruction in a literacy program should allow students to access a variety of texts through four basic modes of reading. Each mode is designed to give students access to texts at either their independent, instructional, or frustration level. The four basic modes are:

1. Read-alouds
2. Shared Reading
3. Guided Reading
4. Independent Reading

Read-Alouds: Learning to Love Reading

Jim Trelease, well known for the *Read-Aloud Handbook* (1995), states that even in this modern technological age, the single most important factor that determines a child's future reading success is being read to.

Reading aloud is modeling for students the joy of reading. You can also build background for informational reading, model good reading fluency and intonation, and provide access to text above the levels and abilities of students in your classes.

It can be a brief time, and it can be something as simple as an article from last night's paper that you found interesting and want to share with students. It can be ongoing, such as a time when you read a novel with students for 10 minutes a day. There really are no rules for what is shared, other than it should be of interest to you and your students.

HELPFUL HINTS FOR READING ALOUD

- Try to have a regularly scheduled time at least once a week, even if only for 5-10 minutes.
- Select material you like and you think your students will like.
- Vary the type of material read—fiction and nonfiction, short and long, books, magazines, newspapers, etc.
- Avoid books heavy in dialogue, as it is hard for listeners to follow.
- Be familiar with the material, both for good oral delivery and to avoid any problems with language or content.
- If it is a book, have copies for interested students to check out.
- When beginning a text, model predicting and previewing strategies.
- Vary intonational patterns to fit the reading.
- Model think-alouds and questioning the text.
- Stop occasionally and ask students to predict or share common experiences.
- Stop a session at a suspenseful spot, leaving students hanging and wanting more.
- Talk afterward, to give students the opportunity to discuss and react to the literature.

(Sanacore 1996 and Trelease 1995)

Shared Reading: Modeling Expectations

Shared reading is any reading situation in which students:

- listen to the teacher, a tape, a CD, or another expert reader reading with fluency and expression.
- follow that reading in their own copy of the text.
- participate as much as they are able through a variety of strategies.
- discuss the text with the teacher's guidance.

Shared reading allows students to enjoy materials that are above their instructional level and have opportunities to apply what they know to this literature.

The essentials of shared reading are that the teacher explains and/or demonstrates for students the important processes that need to be done while reading. The teacher follows the lead of the students, allowing them to do all the work that they can and stepping in to support the reader when help is needed. Shared reading is needed when children read texts that present new difficulties and require the use of new strategies. In reality, much of what teachers do is to support "thinking" (Cunningham and Allington 2006).

For secondary students, shared reading is the method that helps struggling readers access grade-level text when they cannot read it by themselves. It should not be the central focus of instruction for students who need *Caught Reading*. Rather, it should be used more often in classes like social studies or science, or with the Globe Fearon Literature anthology. Because these texts may be at students' frustration level, modeling effective reading habits is particularly important.

Guided Reading: Learning to Learn, A Gift for Life

Guided reading is the bridge between shared and independent reading. To provide guided reading instruction, use the *Caught Reading* Worktext lessons.

After administering the assessment, students will be placed in their diagnosed instructional range, allowing teachers to build schema for content and thinking processes (Wood, Cunningham and Allington, Mooney, Stanovich). Guided reading also allows students to build confidence as they learn strategies that will enable them to fix problems as they read.

For at-risk students, it is best to work through the materials in small groups, perhaps assigning appropriate independent work or silent reading to part of the class, while the teacher works with the other part. This allows better monitoring of student progress and response.

Remember that *Caught Reading* also includes Midway and Final Novels that can be used in discussion groups to build students' comprehension skills. Because these are designed to be at the same reading level as the Worktext, they become appropriate instructional-range material.

The following are differences of guided reading from shared reading:

- the students read, not the teacher
- the material they are reading is at their instructional range of ability
- for most students, reading is silent, although oral reading may be occasionally done to help you monitor their growth in word recognition
- the teacher actively supports students and guides their reading and questioning strategies

Questions the teacher asks during guided reading should encourage students to construct meaning. Before reading, questions should lead students to the important ideas in the text. In narrative text, they should focus on the setting of the story (time and place), the major characters, the story problem, the action, the resolution, and the overall moral or theme. In expository text, they should focus on the main ideas, author's purpose, and the ability to evaluate fact and opinion and draw logical conclusions.

The *Caught Reading Teacher's Manual* points out the Literature Connection and gives ideas for other appropriate Pearson materials that can be used in a guided reading setting.

Independent Reading: Practicing the Craft of Reading

Independent reading is often known as Silent Sustained Reading (SSR), Drop Everything and Read (DEAR), or some other acronym for time spent reading without direct teacher instruction, often with self-selected books. It is important that students use books at their independent reading level, allowing them to build fluency and find pleasure in reading without struggling, unless they choose to select more difficult books due to keen interest in a topic. Cohen (1999) provides a rationale for including an independent reading component in a reading program. "[Students] can increase their knowledge and understanding of writing, spelling, reading comprehension, and reading speed. When used consistently and reinforced by helping students choose appropriate literature, [independent reading] provides low anxiety practice and support for students still developing their reading skills."

In the *SSR Handbook*, Pilgreen (2000) provides eight factors for success with an independent reading experience.

1. **Access.** The material should be readily available to students.
2. **Appeal.** Students should select their own materials from a wide assortment. The assortment should include a variety of genres, sources, types, and reading levels.
3. **Environment.** Students should have the opportunity to read in a quiet environment without interruptions.
4. **Encouragement.** Teachers should share ideas about books, recommend books, and discuss them with students. Students can also share books they have read with their peers.
5. **Non-accountability.** There should be no book reports or official recordkeeping. Students may choose to self-monitor and track their own performance.
6. **Scheduled reading.** Regularly scheduled, daily reading is best, but students should have the opportunity for independent reading at least twice a week.
7. **Staff training.** Teachers need to learn and share strategies for linking students with books.
8. **Follow-up activities.** The activities should be voluntary and grow out of a desire to share.

Even if it is only a few minutes a day, it adds up. Trelease (1995) reports that by reading 20 minutes a day, six days a week, the average reader would accumulate 104 hours a year and 3,000 pages, equal to four of Dickens's classics.

How Do Teachers Manage Multiple Modes?

Students with reading problems will often create disturbances to avoid the task of reading, especially secondary students with a history of failure. However, students engaged in tasks at their appropriate level of reading, with high expectations and clear routines established, will have fewer of these problems. "When teens know ahead of time what they will be asked to do, and that help will be available when they need it, they feel safe and in control. A program also must make sense to them and provide them hope. They need to know why they have been placed in a particular course of instruction, and more appropriately, what they will be able to do when they complete it" (Curtis and Longo 1999).

- To help make a successful classroom, look at the physical environment.
    1. Are there clear paths through the room?
    2. Are materials placed in convenient spots to avoid congestion and to allow easy accessibility?
    3. Are particular areas of the room designated for specific activities?
    4. Are schedules set and posted so that students know when, why, what, and for how long activities will occur? (Curtis and Longo 1999)

- It is also important to plan a variety of activities, ranging from 5–30 minutes. Research shows that adults cannot sustain interest for more than 20–25 minutes. So, how can we expect our students to do more?

- Students also need to understand that participation in reading routines is a requirement, not an option. Students' participation begins before formal reading does. Prereading is the first step. During prereading, students engage the text through various preliminary steps, such as setting a purpose for reading, tapping their prior knowledge, and previewing their reading. As students begin a formal read of the text, their participation continues with during-reading and postreading strategies. This three-step process encourages active participation and helps to ensure students' connections to and involvement in their reading. For a comprehensive look at each stage in the process, see the chart on page 161 of this *Manual*.

A Process for Reading to Learn

Prereading	During Reading	Postreading
• In prereading, students should: 　–set a purpose for reading. 　–tap prior knowledge. 　–preview and predict what they will read by: 　–identifying key terms. 　–looking at visuals. 　–assessing the level of difficulty and length of what they will read. 　–gaining a general sense of the topic and major subtopics. 　–understanding text organization. 　–determining how this information relates to what they already know.	• During reading, students should: 　–look for key concepts and main ideas. 　–make inferences and check them. 　–monitor comprehension by: 　–thinking about what they have read. 　–talking back to the text. 　–using vocabulary techniques to understand new words. 　–relating each paragraph to the selection's main point. 　–taking good notes.	• Just after reading, students should: 　–review what they have read by writing a summary. 　–relate what they read to what they already know. 　–create a graphic organizer. 　–revisit predictions. 　–solve a problem. 　–adjust information they gathered when previewing. 　–confirm key concepts. 　–reread, if necessary.

Five Major Categories of Skill Instruction

Every lesson in the *Caught Reading* program provides opportunities for reading, as well as skill instruction in all the major categories. The major categories are: Word Attack, Spelling, Vocabulary Development, Fluency, and Comprehension. To maximize the effectiveness of this instruction, teachers need feedback from student performance so that they may modify the pacing, focus, or manner of delivery as needed.

Caught Reading provides assessment at three stages in the program. Both formal and informal measures are used.

Stage I: Preassessment

Stage II: Ongoing Assessment (Progress Monitoring)

Stage III: Postassessment

The following is a description of how and when feedback is provided for each of the reading skills and strategies.

Category 1: Word Attack

The skilled reader has a number of strategies for recognizing unfamiliar words at his or her disposal. Mastering these Word Attack strategies is essential to fluent reading.

The *Caught Reading* program provides explicit instruction and assessment for three different types of Word Attack strategies: phonic analysis, structural analysis, and contextual analysis.

1. Phonic analysis

Readers break unfamiliar words down using letter/sound correspondences. Words are sounded out letter-by-letter or by using spelling patterns. Readers may also use analogy, or comparing patterns with words they already know.

example: "all;" you know the word "all." Add the letter "c" to the word, and you have "call."

Instruction

Phonic analysis is presented in every skill-based lesson throughout Levels 1–7 of the *Caught Reading* program. It always appears as the first Word Attack section in the lesson before the Words to Know.

Preassessment

The Elementary Spelling Inventory I is designed to provide specific feedback about students' phonic analysis skills.

Ongoing Assessment

The *Caught Reading* Practice Lessons, located in Worktexts 1–7, provide teachers with an informal method to monitor students' skills. Teachers may also monitor students' oral reading for clues to Word Attack problems.

2. Structural analysis

Readers break unfamiliar words down into word parts—roots, prefixes, suffixes, and the combining forms of compound words. This may also be referred to as morphological analysis.

example: thinking = think + ing
           firetruck = fire + truck

Instruction
Structural analysis is also presented in every skill-based lesson throughout the program. It is the second Word Attack section in each of these lessons and occurs after the Words to Know.

Preassessment
The Elementary Spelling Inventory I is designed to provide specific feedback about students' structural analysis skills.

Ongoing Assessment
The Practice and Assessment booklets that accompany each Level of the program provide teachers with an informal method to monitor students' skills. Teachers may also monitor students' oral reading for clues to Word Attack problems.

3. Contextual analysis

Readers use context words surrounding the unknown word to help determine its meaning.

example: The cook is in the kitchen.
           Students begin by phonic analysis "kitch-en" and use
               the context (cook) to confirm.

Instruction
Contextual analysis is first taught in Level 3 and continues on in higher levels. It appears under the heading Take a Guess.

Preassessment
Teachers may monitor students' oral reading of test passages for clues to Word Attack problems.

Ongoing Assessment
Teachers may monitor students' oral reading for clues to Word Attack problems.

Category 2: Spelling

Spelling skills, or the ability to encode speech into the written word, are intimately linked with Word Attack skills, or the ability to decode the written word into speech. They should be developed simultaneously, and they can reinforce one another. However, not all good readers, or decoders, are good spellers, or encoders. Therefore, it is critical to include specific spelling instruction as part of any reading program. The development of this skill should be monitored and assessed just as decoding and comprehension skills are.

Developmental Stages of Spelling

Words Their Way (Bear et al 2003) defines five stages of spelling development, which tend to correspond to the stages of reading development. The five stages are: emergent, letter name-alphabetic, within word pattern, syllables and affixes, and derivational relations. Most secondary students are in the last three stages. For a comprehensive look at each of the stages and their corresponding characteristics, see page 165 of this *Manual*.

Instruction

Spelling is taught in every skill-based lesson in several ways. The "Words to Know" section includes a four-step process for reinforcing spelling. The Look-Say-Picture-Write sequence encourages students' visual recognition of vocabulary words, helps them develop a broader sight vocabulary, and focuses their attention on the form or spelling of the words. Finally, the Word Attack sections in the lessons teach and reinforce spelling skills on a continuous basis. Spelling rules are often presented explicitly in these sections, and students have an opportunity to practice what they have learned.

Preassessment

The Elementary Spelling Inventory I included in this book helps teachers diagnose spelling difficulties and provides a greater understanding of students' decoding abilities.

Ongoing Assessment

Teachers may monitor students' performance in the Words to Know section of their Worktext lessons, as well as in the writing activities in the Practice Lessons. They may also administer the Elementary Spelling Inventory I several times during the year (three times a year is recommended), as a way to monitor students' progress.

The Five Stages of Spelling Development

Emergent	Letter Name-Alphabetic
Characteristics: • Scribbles letters and numbers • Lacks concept of a word • Lacks letter-sound correspondence • Pretends to read and write	**Characteristics:** • Beginning consonants • Vowel in each word • Short vowels spelled correctly • Understand that syllables have vowels • Through wide reading, learns high frequency words • Initial consonant digraphs and blends

Within Word Pattern	Syllables and Affixes	Derivational Relations

Characteristics:
• Approaching fluency
• Correct spelling in words with "m" or "n" like "bump" or "bunch" (nasals)—hallmark of this stage
• Most single syllable short vowel words
• Long vowel patterns
• Consonant blends and digraphs
• Can read low-frequency vowel words they cannot spell
• Most other, more abstract, vowel patterns
• Patterns do not always have to be consistent with sound
	Characteristics:
	• Syllables meet at their juncture
	• Begin polysyllabic words
	• Begin consonant doubling principle, from "clopped" to "settle" or "occasion"
	• Inflectional endings added correctly to base words
	• Less frequent prefixes and suffixes spelled correctly
	• Begin to see connections between spelling and syntax
	  –tion/sion
	  –change verbs into nouns: er/or/ian
	• Importance of accents and stress syllables for syntax and semantics
	  –You signed the contract.
	  –He may contract the disease.
	• Spelling-meaning connection, increasing vocabulary simultaneously
		Characteristics:
		• Words from derived forms spelled correctly
		• Examine how words share common derivations and related roots and bases
		• Discover that meaning and spelling of parts of words remain constant across different words
		  –trans: "transportation," "transport," "transplant," "transmit"
		• Learn history of words and their derivations
		• Word study shows how spelling tells them meaning/pronunciation blurs meaning, e.g.:
		  –"competition" spelled as "composition"=look at "compete" as the base
		  –"composition" spelled as "compusition"=look at "compose"

Spelling Activities

The following activities are designed to reinforce spelling skills. Teachers may use these in addition to activities found in the *Caught Reading Teacher's Manual* and Worktexts.

1. Dictation Game

Students work in pairs to dictate and record new vocabulary words from their lessons.

Materials:
- *Caught Reading* Worktexts. Use the Words to Know from the current lesson or the corresponding Memory Chips from the back of the book. Memory Chips are tear-out word cards found in the back of each student Worktext, Levels 1–7. The front of each card has a word from the lesson presented in context. The back has the word in isolation.
- blank paper and pencil

Procedure:
- Students divide into pairs and use the Words to Know from their Worktext lesson for dictation. One reads and the other writes. Students take turns in both roles.
- One partner may also read the dictated words, while the other partner finds that word's Memory Chip and displays it.

2. Making Sentences

Students make words and sentences using letter and phonogram chips.

Materials:
- letter and phonogram chips, which are commercially available or teacher-created
- Phonograms: ack, ad, ail, ain, ake, all, an, ank, ap, are, at, ave, ay, ear, eat, ed, ell, en, et, ice, ick, id, ide, light, ill, in, ing, ip, it, old, op, ore, ow, to, up, ut.

Procedure:
- Display a group of phonogram chips on a table like playing cards. Begin with one chip, then ask students to take turns selecting chips from the group to add to the first one until a complete sentence is built.
- Students select a phonogram and make as many verbs as possible. Then, they try making as many nouns, adjectives, and adverbs as possible.

3. Bingo

This activity provides two opportunities for the students to spell and recognize words correctly. It can be played with a whole class or in small groups.

Materials:
- game cards (Use the reproducible on page 167 of this *Manual* or ask students to create their own game cards.)
- Bingo chips (can be anything to cover spaces on a board)

Procedure:
- Each student gets or creates a bingo game card.
- The teacher dictates 24 words for the game from the High Frequency Words Assessments or from the Worktext Words to Know.
- Students randomly write the words in any square of their game card.
- The teacher calls out one word at a time, while students place a marker over that word on their game card.
- The first student who has a row or column of words covered calls "BINGO!"

WORD BINGO

		FREE		

4. Word Scramble

Students working in pairs have three minutes to make words by sorting the letters and creating one- to six-letter words from the letter squares.

Materials:
- letter squares (commercially available or teacher-made)
- sand clock or timer
- recording sheet (see below) and pencil

Procedure:
- Students work in pairs. They assign roles: One is the recorder and the other is the word maker. Each pair should draw their recording chart to look like the one below.
- Each pair of students gets a determined number of letter squares to spread out in front of them.
- The timer is set for three minutes.
- The word maker makes as many two-, three-, four-, five-, or six-letter words as possible, using only the letters available.
- As the words are made, the recorder writes them in the appropriate column and immediately puts the letters back in the pile to be used again.
- At the end of the three minutes, the word maker reads all the words back to the recorder, who checks for accuracy of spelling.
- One point is given for each letter. Students count up and record the total number of points scored. The pair with the most number of points wins. If a word is misspelled, no points are given.
- If a pair of students are playing alone, they alternate turns, and the player with the most points wins.

Word Scramble Recording Sheet

1-letter word	2-letter word	3-letter word	4-letter word	5-letter word	6-letter word

Total Points _____

Category 3: Vocabulary Development

Vocabulary development is an essential component of a reading program. Without a broad vocabulary base, students will have difficulty comprehending the types of texts they will encounter in school, at work, and in their daily lives. "Numerous researchers have noted that poor readers have smaller vocabularies than good readers. Indeed, vocabulary knowledge is one of the best single predictors of reading comprehension" (Daneman 1991). Because struggling readers usually read less than better readers, their skills in vocabulary develop correspondingly slower.

Beyond extensive reading, a comprehensive vocabulary development program that meets the needs of diverse students should:

- teach words that are essential to academic success and not acquired independently.
- include systematic procedures to make students independent word learners.
- include teaching that is active, hands-on, and directed at assessed student needs, helping students to internalize strategies.

Students need multiple exposures to words and multiple opportunities to practice using words. When new information is connected in meaningful ways with previously learned information, it is more likely to become part of students' permanent bank of knowledge. In vocabulary development, this occurs:

- by having students practice words whose meanings they have learned in multiple subject areas or learning contexts; and
- by systematically building new word knowledge on previous word knowledge (Baker et al 1998).

Instruction

In *Caught Reading,* each Level provides several opportunities to work with a defined set of vocabulary words, the Words to Know. Students complete a four-step Look–Say–Picture–Write process to reinforce the words. They also have immediate opportunities to see the words in context in the lesson's story. This vocabulary is reinforced in the next free lesson where students again read the new words in the context of a high-interest story.

Tear-out Memory Chips also appear at the back of each Worktext. These miniature flash cards contain all of the vocabulary taught in the Level. On the front of the card, the word appears in context. On the back, it appears in isolation. Students may practice with these Memory Chips on their own or with a partner. Suggestions are given in the *Caught Reading Teacher's Manual.*

The *Caught Reading Teacher's Manual* also includes reteaching suggestions in subsequent lessons. Teachers may also continue to reinforce vocabulary development using other tools, such as word-study notebooks and word walls.

Vocabulary strategies and the activities and strategies discussed in the spelling section go hand in hand. Working with words in a variety of ways helps build students' vocabulary knowledge as they actively sort, identify, and develop words, word lists, word banks, and word notebooks. These provide multiple contacts with the words and help students use them in meaningful ways. The more students are exposed to a word that occurs in a meaningful context, the higher the chance of students using and understanding the word as part of their regular vocabulary.

Preassessment

Vocabulary development is preassessed in the questions that follow the Initial Filter Passage and Level Passages. Among the comprehension questions, there are always questions focusing on word meaning. These questions are designed to give teachers feedback regarding students' vocabulary development.

Ongoing Assessment

Teachers may choose to monitor students' progress by several means. They may collect and review the Words to Know exercises in the Worktext. They may also observe students working with their Memory Chips to help determine if they are having problems. Finally, they may listen to students' oral reading. If students stumble over particular words, it may mean that they do not understand these words.

Vocabulary Development Activities

1. The Teacher's Cat

This is a word game that asks students to suggest words in a particular category.

Materials: beanbag or rubber ball

Procedure:
- The teacher holds the beanbag and starts the game with a sentence:

    "The teacher's cat is a fat (or any adjective here) cat."

- The teacher tosses the ball to someone in the class.
- The student who catches the ball must come up with his or her own sentence, filling in the blank with another adjective that starts with "f" (or whatever the first letter of the first word chosen was).

    "The teacher's cat is a frugal (or any adjective here) cat."

- After the student says his or her word, he or she tosses the beanbag to a classmate. The game continues as students continue tossing the beanbag and creating sentences.
- At any point as agreed upon by the class, a new word can be introduced, starting with a different letter.

2. Word Rings

Students make "word rings" for reviewing words with which they are having trouble. They may also use the Memory Chips in the Worktexts.

Materials:
- binder lock rings or string/ribbon/yarn to hold cards together
- index cards

Procedure:
- Students print the words on one side of the card, one word per card. The words can be ones that they have been missing in the High Frequency Words Assessments.
- On the back of the card, students use the word in a sentence that demonstrates its meaning, underlining the target word.
- Students can then punch a hole in the top corner of each card and put them on a ring or string.
- Mastered words can be discarded. New ones can be added as needed.

3. Hink Pinks

This is a rhyming game that has been around for many years. Students think of pairs of one syllable words that rhyme, such as *fat cat*, and then create definitions for each word. Hinky Pinkies is the same game using two syllable words.

Materials: Recording Sheet (Use the one below as a model.)

Procedure:
- Students work in pairs to come up with rhyming words and their definitions. Use the sample below to get them started. They may use a thesaurus to help them.
- They give their Hink Pinks clues to another group to see if they can figure out the answers.

Hink Pinks	
Rhyming Word Pair	**Definition Clue**
fat cat	1. chubby feline
school rule	2. classroom regulation
cheap jeep	3. inexpensive army vehicle
book crook	4. library thief
wrench bench	5. tool holder
	6.
	7.
	8.
	9.
	10.

Hinky Pinkies	
Rhyming Word Pair	**Definition Clue**
handy candy	1. convenient sweets
paper scraper	2. wall covering remover
marriage carriage	3. wedding car
pretty kitty	4. beautiful cat
Navy gravy	5. military meat sauce
	6.
	7.
	8.
	9.
	10.

Category 4: Fluency

Fluency is the ability to read with automaticity and with expression. Automaticity relates to reading rate, or the speed at which the reader reads. However, speed without comprehension is meaningless. Therefore, the "with expression" part of the definition relates to the comprehension of the meaning and intent of the reading selection.

Clearly, comprehension, word recognition, and vocabulary skills underlie fluency. It is not a skill that can be developed in isolation.

Fluency development is generally divided into two categories: reading rate and word recognition. Both of these are important components of the reading process. As students become fluent readers, they use less energy for decoding and more energy for understanding what they read. Good reading skills enhance content and strategy knowledge as well as motivation.

Direct instruction of fluency strategies can help students move toward automaticity earlier and faster. It is critical to detect difficulties and provide early intervention for all students. Improving the ability to read fast, with comprehension, increases overall reading ability and educational success.

Reading Rate (with Comprehension)

Not all good readers read at the same rate. According to Cuomo (1962), the average adult reads about 250 words per minute, with this rate varying from 125 to 900. That's a pretty wide range! Even a single reader will vary his or her reading rate depending upon the complexity of the material he or she is reading. The reason for this variance is that rate alone is not the key to fluency. Readers must comprehend what they are reading as well. Speed without comprehension is not a valuable skill.

There are general benchmarks for reading rate that have been established. Keep in mind, however, that variance is normal. Below are benchmarks for both silent and oral reading.

Silent Reading Rates for Students in Grades 1–8 Who Understand the Material								
Grade	1	2	3	4	5	6	7	8
WPM	<81	82–108	109–130	131–147	148–161	162–174	175–185	186–197

Median Oral Reading Rates for Students in Grades 2–5 Measured at the End of the School Year (Hasbrouck and Tindal 1992)				
Grade	2	3	4	5
WPM	94–124	114–142	118–143	128–151

A person with a rate of less than 100 words per minute almost always reads word by word. This method is so slow and inefficient that it actually hinders comprehension. Cuomo (1962) suggested that students who cannot read text at 100 words per minute with 95 percent accuracy by the end of third grade would have a difficult time keeping up with assigned reading.

Instruction

Of course, it is impossible to teach fluency independently. It is the by-product of automaticity in word recognition, vocabulary knowledge, decoding skills, and higher-order comprehension skills, and so must be taught by reading in context. Teachers can, however, explain the concept and model fluent reading for students with read-alouds. Teachers can also provide frequent opportunities for students to read materials that will help them develop fluency. Decodable texts are among the most important of these materials. It is very important for teachers to perform frequent assessments as well to monitor their students' gains.

Most experts agree that decodable texts are an important tool for the development of fluency. Decodable texts contain only the words students are able to decode at their instructional level. This enables students to spend less time struggling to decode and more time focusing on the meaning of the text. Remember, comprehension is critical for fluency. *Caught Reading* provides many opportunities for students to read decodable text.

Skill Lessons in Worktexts. Teachers may elect to read the stories in these lessons aloud to model fluent reading. They may also choose to read from other materials such as newspapers, magazines, or novels to engage student interest in the reading process.

Free Lessons in Worktexts. All the lessons in the Worktexts have a story that is constructed with only the words that students have been taught up to that point. Every other one of these lessons is a free lesson in which students do not learn any new skills, but simply practice fluency by reading a new high-interest story.

Midway and Final Novels. Each Worktext has two accompanying novels. One is meant to be read midway through the Worktext. The other is to be read at the end of the Worktext. Both are 100 percent decodable and are designed to be read independently.

Hi/Lo Readers. Beginning in Level 3, recommendations are made in the *Caught Reading Teacher's Manual* for students to begin using high-interest, low-reading level readers. Pearson publishes dozens of series of various genres at different reading levels.

Preassessment

Reading rate can alert teachers to potential problems. Any student reading below 100 words per minute is likely to need to spend more time reading (decodable texts to begin with and independent reading using hi/lo readers later on, for example).

Ongoing Assessment

Fluency Checks. Three timed fluency checks are recommended for each of the seven Levels of the program. Have students monitor their own results. The words per minute should increase for students from check to check. Each passage is accompanied by 5–10 comprehension questions to ensure that students continue to read for understanding.

Decodable Novels. Comprehension questions for the two decodable novels that accompany each Level of *Caught Reading* (Midway Novel and Final Novel) can be found in the *Teacher's Manual*. Teachers may use these to ensure that students are reading the novels with understanding.

Oral Reading. Teachers may choose to observe students' oral reading as an informal method of monitoring fluency.

Word Recognition and High Frequency Words

The second component of fluency is word recognition. Word recognition is the ability to identify words automatically, without having to "sound them out." Automaticity in word recognition is necessary for fast reading rates.

Word recognition and speed are not just products of skillful reading—they are necessary for it to happen (Adams 1990). To read books, students need to be able to read words quickly and automatically. If a child stumbles over or has to decode too many words slowly, comprehension will suffer (Samuels, Schermer, and Reinking 1992).

Although teachers want students to have a strategy for decoding words they do not know, they also want them to recognize many words automatically and be able to read them in context. High-frequency words are so common in reading materials that children must learn to identify them (Tompkins 2005). Students who recognize many high-frequency words are able to read more fluently than those who do not, and fluent readers are better able to understand what they are reading.

Instruction

Caught Reading includes several methods for practicing word recognition.

- **Words to Know.** The Words to Know section of each skill-based lesson includes a four-step process designed to help students recognize words by sight. The steps include Look–Say–Picture–Write. This process reinforces visual features of words and connects them with the sound and meaning of the word.

- **Memory Chips.** These tear-out miniature flash cards are located at the back of each student Worktext. Every word taught in the series has a card. Students can practice alone or in pairs. There are also several teacher-directed activities included in the *Caught Reading Teacher's Manual*.

Ongoing Assessment

On pages 131–137 of this *Manual* there are several High Frequency Words Quizzes. Students are required to study the words on the lists until they are mastered for the posttest. However, because performance on the tests is not enough, they will also be required to spell those words correctly in all future writing. Mastery of the words assigned to each Level is necessary before exiting that Level and moving on in the program.

In selecting the words for this process, vocabulary lists for each Level were compared to the Dolch List and Fry's first 600 Essential Words through 4th grade. There are seven lists of words for each Level, which can be used for the process outlined in the Assessment directions. These lists are composed of (1) vocabulary words from each Level, excluding proper nouns, selection-specific words not considered to be high frequency, and words repeated from a prior level and (2) words from the Dolch and Fry lists that do not appear in *Caught Reading* vocabulary lists, but many of which appear in the reading selections.

Tips for Improving Fluency (Robb 2000)

- Designate a private, quiet area of the classroom as a place where students can try repeated readings, listen to recorded stories, and practice reading poetry or a reader's theater script.
- Students can also record themselves—once in the beginning of the year and several times during the year so they can have proof of improvement and establish goals for improvement. This is an excellent tool for parent conferences.
- In Echo-read poetry, the teacher reads one or two lines, then students read the same lines, following the teacher's rhythm and inflection.
- Memorize poetry and recite it for an audience selected by the student.
- Present short plays or reader's theater scripts.

Fluency Activities

1. Rereadings

Samuel's research (1976/1997) on repeated readings likens readers to athletes who spend great amounts of time practicing such skills as dribbling, hitting, throwing balls, jumping, or working to develop speed and smoothness.

Dowhower (1987) suggests using short passages from text in the student's instructional range. As the student's speed and accuracy reaches acceptable levels, the difficulty level of the passage can increase. In the *Caught Reading* curriculum, students can reread the passages used for Fluency Checks, working to increase their speed. Students can keep records of their reading rate as proof of growth, as well as motivation for practice.

2. Paired Repeated Reading (Wood 1992)

Working in pairs, students select their own passage approximately 50 words in length from material currently being used for instruction.

- Each student reads his or her own passage silently, then decides who will read aloud first.
- The first reader reads the passage aloud three times, evaluating his or her own reading on a scale of 1–4, with 4 being the highest.
- After the second and third reading, the listener tells how the reading improved, i.e., more smoothly, with expression, etc. You may wish to develop a checklist with students that they could use for this activity.
- After the third reading, partners switch roles and repeat the process.

3. Book Pass (Allen 2000)

Use this strategy about once a month to help students make appropriate selections of books for silent reading. Provide independent reading materials from your class library. (Pearson offers many hi/lo readers appropriate for your library.)

Procedure

- Gather enough books so that each student can have one.
- Put student desks or chairs in a circle or designate the "path" for books to be circulated around the room.
- Model how you sample a book before deciding to read it, filling in the form on page 178 of this *Manual*.
- Randomly distribute books and Book Pass worksheets to every student.
- Remind students that they should look at the cover, read the beginning, and quickly sample the book.
- After one to two minutes, call "book pass," and ask students to fill in the worksheet. Then, ask students to pass the book in the designated direction.
- Continue this process for at least five or six turns, gradually increasing the time throughout the year so all students view all books.
- At the end, ask for any comments students may want to make about a particular book. Prompt this with questions like "Did anyone find a book they can't wait to read?" or "Did anyone find a book to recommend to a friend?"
- When finished, students should put the forms in their folders or notebooks for future reference in choosing books.

TITLE	AUTHOR	COMMENTS

Category 5: Comprehension

Comprehension is the end goal of all reading. Word Attack, vocabulary, spelling, and fluency are all developed to the point of automaticity to allow the reader to devote his or her energy to understanding the meaning and purpose of the text. Yet comprehension skills themselves may be explicitly taught as well.

There are three general levels of comprehension skills. Each level becomes increasingly more complex and each builds upon the previous level.

- **Literal.** This type of comprehension skill involves understanding exactly and only what the text says.
- **Inferential.** This skill involves understanding what the text implies but may not say explicitly.
- **Critical.** Critical comprehension involves being able to evaluate the text for point of view, purpose, accuracy, value, and truthfulness.

Instruction

Comprehension is a major strand of the *Caught Reading* program. Every lesson, whether it is a skill-based or free lesson, provides practice with multiple levels of comprehension. Students also have the opportunity to work in groups and share ideas.

As students grow from "learning to read" to "reading to learn," the types of texts they read change. They generally move from simple, narrative texts to more complex, academic expository texts. Thus, the focus of the comprehension skills they employ must change as well. *Caught Reading* follows students through this transition, starting with Level 4, and begins to introduce content-area skills and strategies as students are ready for them.

Preassessment

Student comprehension skills are assessed throughout the Preassessment process. The Initial Filter and Level Pretests both contain a comprehension component. All three levels of comprehension—literal, inferential, and critical—are assessed and clearly identified for teachers in the corresponding answer keys.

Ongoing Assessment

There are many opportunities for teachers to monitor students' comprehension throughout the *Caught Reading* program. These include both formal and informal measures.

- **Worktext Lesson Comprehension Questions.** Teachers can monitor students' performance either orally or in writing.
- **Midway and Final Novel Comprehension Questions.** These questions appear in the *Caught Reading Teacher's Manual*. Teachers can monitor students' performance by having them answer questions either orally or in writing.

Comprehension Activities

1. Think-Alouds

Thinking aloud while reading is one instructional tool teachers can use to make the ordinarily hidden mental processes of reading visible, to model the process of making sense of texts, to demonstrate the comprehension problems all readers face, and to make apparent the variety of problem-solving strategies proficient readers employ.

Reading for Understanding (Schoenbach et al 1999), a powerful tool for teaching comprehension strategies, describes the following process for teaching the Think-Aloud process:

Step 1: Model the Think-Aloud Process outlined below while reading a passage that you have not previously seen. Read the passage aloud while modeling. Put it on an overhead or handout so students can follow along. Make the distinction clear between reading aloud and thinking aloud, perhaps pausing, looking away from the text, and changing body posture.

Step 2: After a few demonstrations, ask students to use a checklist to identify your processes. This process helps the students zero in on a variety of strategies. Students make a tally mark each time they hear one of the cues.

Step 3: After several opportunities to hear and monitor your modeling, have students practice the strategy with a partner, using the same checklist.

Step 4: Ask students to practice the strategy individually and silently, paying attention to their thoughts and using the checklist for their own thinking. Ask them to share and reflect on their processes.

Step 5: For ongoing practice/application, have students keep a folder for their tallies with a variety of genres and assess their own progress periodically. Continue to model this process with a variety of texts as they are introduced during the year.

Think-Aloud Process
Predicting   I predict...; In the next part I think...; I think this is...
Picturing   I picture...; I can see...
Making Connections   This is like a...; This reminds me of...
Identifying a Problem   I got confused when...; I'm not sure of...; I didn't expect...
Using Fixups   I think I'll have to (reread/take some other action to comprehend); Maybe I'll need to (read on, etc.)

2. Alphaboxes: A Reflective Strategy (Hoyt 1998)

After reading, students work in pairs or small groups to think of words that reflect important points in the selection. They put their words into the appropriate box on the form on page 181 of this *Manual*, making sure they can tell how each word relates to the story. A class list can also be made of the most interesting words generated by the groups, making sure students provide justification.

ALPHABOXES

The Book/Story _____

The Reader(s) _____

A	B	C	D
E	F	G	H
I	J	K	L
M	N	O	P
Q	R	S	T
U	V	W	XYZ

Assessment Charts

The Assessment Charts in this section have been designed to facilitate the recording of assessment results. You will use some of the charts, while other charts have been designed for student use. By having students take part in the grading and recording of the results, (1) students are encouraged to take a more active role in their reading-skills development, and (2) the time it takes you to grade and record results will be drastically reduced.

The Assessment Charts in this section include: a Quick Placement Recording Chart, a Student Diagnostic Chart, an Error Guide for Elementary Spelling Inventory I, a Feature Guide for Elementary Spelling Inventory I, Individual Student Monthly Progress Monitoring Chart for *Caught Reading* (Academic Year), Individual Student Monthly Progress Monitoring Chart for *Caught Reading* (Full Calendar Year), Monthly Class Summary Chart, Fluency Check Student Recording Chart (Levels 1–3), Fluency Check Student Recording Chart (Levels 4–7), and a High Frequency Words Mastery Chart.

For more information about when and how to use each of the charts, read the Administration Procedure that accompanies each assessment provided in this *Manual.*

Caught Reading Quick Placement Recording Chart

Administer passages as needed. Record data and use to place students.

Student Name	Score for Initial Filter	Place in Be A Better Reader?	Score for Levels 4 and 5 Passages	Individual Assessment	Caught Reading Placement Level
	90% or better → Be A Better Reader **less than 90%** → continue assessment	**Yes** → discontinue assessment **No** → move to Passages 4 and 5	**55% or better** → determine placement **50% or less** → continue assessment	**Yes** → continue assessment **No** → determine placement	Record final placement level here

Number of students in *Be A Better Reader: Starting Out* _____ Number of students in *Be A Better Reader: Level A* _____

Number of students in *Caught Reading*:

Getting Ready ____	Level 1 ____	Level 2 ____	Level 3 ____
Level 4 ____	Level 5 ____	Level 6 ____	Level 7 ____

Student Diagnostic Chart

Name _____ Period _____ Beginning Date _____

LEVEL PRETESTS			ELEMENTARY SPELLING INVENTORY I			NAMES TEST OF DECODING	FLUENCY CHECKS	
Score all applicable passages, record number of correct answers for the five types of questions			Score test and determine spelling stage			(if applicable) Record errors in each category (Total possible)	Calculate silent reading rate and compare to norms as given below	
Questions • Type of question • Number of question	Number Correct		Spelling Stage	Recommendations for Instruction			Grade Level Norms for Silent Reading	
							Reading Rate	Grade Level
• Recall • Numbers 1–5			Early Letter Name	• Focus on High Frequency Words and phonemic awareness		Initial Consonants (37)	<81	
						Initial Consonant Blends (19)		
• Vocabulary • Number 6			Within Word	• Check proficiency on High Frequency Words • Plan activities for Within Word strategies		Consonant Digraphs (15)	82–108	
						Short Vowels (36)		
• Topic • Number 7			Syllable Affix	• Check proficiency on High Frequency Words • Focus on *Caught Reading* spelling rules—word patterns, roots, affixes, etc.		Long Vowels/VC final e (23)	109–130	
• Inference • Numbers 8–9						Vowel Digraphs (15)	131–147	
• Evaluation • Number 10						Controlled Vowels (25)	148–161	
						Schwa (15)	162–174	
Use data to determine focus of comprehension instruction.			Use data to determine focus of spelling instruction			Use data to help students set goals for ongoing Fluency Checks.	175–185	
							186–197	
							Use data to determine focus of phonics instruction.	

© Pearson Education, Inc. or its affiliate(s). All rights reserved.

Error Guide for Elementary Spelling Inventory I

Directions: Circle student's spelling attempts below. If a spelling is not listed, write it where it belongs on the developmental continuum. Circle spelling stage that summarizes the student's development.

Student's Name _____ Teacher _____ Grade _____ Date _____

Number spelled correctly: _____
Number of words attempted: _____

Features	Consonants Initial Final	Short Vowels	Digraphs and Blends	Long Vowel Patterns	Other Vowel Patterns	Syllable Junctures / Consonant Doubling / Inflected Endings / Prefixes / Suffixes	Bases and Roots
	EMERGENT	LETTER NAME-ALPHABETIC		WITHIN WORD PATTERN		SYLLABLES & AFFIXES	DERIVATIONAL RELATIONS
SPELLING STAGES	MIDDLE / LATE	EARLY / MIDDLE / LATE		EARLY / MIDDLE / LATE		EARLY / MIDDLE / LATE	EARLY / MIDDLE / LATE
1 bed	b / bd	bad / **bed**					
2 ship	s sp / shp	sep / shep / **ship**					
3 when	w yn / wn	wan / whan / **when**					
4 lump	l lp / lmp	lop / lomp / **lump**					
5 float	f ft vt / fft	fot / flot / flott	flowt / floaut flote / **float**				
6 train	j t / trn	jran / chran / tan tran	teran / traen / **train**				
7 place	p ps / pls	pas / pas palac plas / plac	pase / plais / plase **place**				
8 drive	d j jrv / drf	drv / griv / jriv driv	jrive / drieve / draive **drive**				
9 bright	b bt / brt	bit / brit	bite / brite / briete **bright**				
10 shopping	s sp spg / shp	sapg / sopn shapng	shopn sopen / sopin / shopen shopin **shopping**		shoping / **shopping**		
11 spoil			spol / sole / sool spoyle spole **spoil**		spoal / **spoil**		
12 serving			sefng srvng / srbving sering serfing / surving serveing		serving / **serving**		
13 chewed			cud cooed / cued coyed chued chood		chowd choud **chewed**		
14 carries			cuwed / keres / cares carres carise carys cairries carrys		**carries**		
15 marched			/ much march marchet / marchd		marcht **marched**		
16 shower			/ shewr showr shour shawer / shoer		shouer **shower**		
17 cattle			/ catl cadol / catel		cattle / **cattle**		
18 favor			/ favr faver / favir		**favor**		
19 ripen			ribn / ripn / ripun		ripan ripon / ripen		
20 cellar			/ salr selr celr / salar seler		seller **cellar** / **cellar**		
21 pleasure			/ plasr plager plejer pleser / plesher		plesour **pleasure** / pleasure		
22 fortunate			/ forhnat frehnit foohinit / forchenut fochininte		fortunet / **fortunate**		
23 confident						confadent confedint confedent confedent / confiadent confiednet confiednet confedent confedent / **confident**	
24 civilize						sivils sevelies sivilicse cifillazas sivelize / sivalize civalise civilise **civilize**	
25 opposition						opasion opasishan opozcison opishien oposition / oppassishion opasitian opasition oposision **opposition**	

Feature Guide for Elementary Spelling Inventory I

Student's Name _____ Teacher _____ Grade _____ Date _____ Total Points _____

	EMERGENT LATE	LETTER NAME-ALPHABETIC EARLY MIDDLE LATE		WITHIN WORD PATTERN EARLY MIDDLE LATE		SYLLABLES & AFFIXES EARLY MIDDLE LATE	DERIVATIONAL EARLY	RELATIONS	
	Consonants Initial / Final 2 / 6	Short Vowels 5	Digraphs and Blends 13	Long Vowel Patterns 5	Other Vowel Patterns 6	Syllable Junctures / Consonant Doubling / Inflected Endings / Prefixes / Suffixes 24	Bases and Roots	Word	Points /66
1 bed	b / d	e						bed	
2 ship	/ p	i	sh					ship	
3 when	/ n	e	wh					when	
4 lump	l /	u	mp					lump	
5 float	/ t		fl	oa				float	
6 train	/ n		tr	ai				train	
7 place			pl	a-e				place	
8 drive	/ v		dr	i-e				drive	
9 bright			br	igh				bright	
10 shopping		o	sh			pp / ing		shopping	
11 spoil			sp		oi			spoil	
12 serving					er	ing		serving	
13 chewed			ch		ew	ed		chewed	
14 carries						rr / ies		carries	
15 marched			ch		ar	ed		marched	
16 shower			sh		ow	er		shower	
17 cattle						tt / le		cattle	
18 favor						av / or		favor	
19 ripen						ip / en		ripen	
20 cellar						ll / ar		cellar	
21 pleasure						ure	pleas	pleasure	
22 fortunate					or	ate	fortun	fortunate	
23 confident						con / ent	fid	confident	
24 civilize						ize	civil	civilize	
25 opposition						op / pp / tion	pos	opposition	
feature totals									

© Pearson Education, Inc. or its affiliate(s). All rights reserved.

Individual Student Monthly Progress Monitoring Chart for *Caught Reading* (Academic Year)

Student's Name _____

	SEPT.	OCT.	NOV.	DEC.	JAN.	FEB.	MARCH	APRIL	MAY	JUNE
	Student assessment within Levels. Record information for all Levels in which a student works during the year.									Final Summary—Next Steps
Caught Reading Level	___% correct	___% correct	___% correct	___% correct	___% correct	___% correct	___% correct	___% correct	___% correct	
After Midway Novel: Comprehension Check (TM)	___% correct	___% correct	___% correct	___% correct	___% correct	___% correct	___% correct	___% correct	___% correct	
After Midway Novel: Midway Assessment (page ___)	___% correct	___% correct	___% correct	___% correct	___% correct	___% correct	___% correct	___% correct	___% correct	
Average scores during month for Practice Lessons	___% correct	___% correct	___% correct	___% correct	___% correct	___% correct	___% correct	___% correct	___% correct	
After Final Novel: Comprehension Check (TM)	___% correct	___% correct	___% correct	___% correct	___% correct	___% correct	___% correct	___% correct	___% correct	
After Final Novel: Final Assessment (page ___)	___% correct	___% correct	___% correct	___% correct	___% correct	___% correct	___% correct	___% correct	___% correct	
	Stop and Look! What does student know/is student able to do?									
	Student assessment beyond Worktext/Levels									
Highest Fluency Check for month/ WPM+comp. score	WPM = ___ Score	WPM = ___ Score	WPM = ___ Score	WPM = ___ Score	WPM = ___ Score	WPM = ___ Score	WPM = ___ Score	WPM = ___ Score	WPM = ___ Score	WPM = ___ Score
High Frequency Words: % correct	___% correct	___% correct	___% correct	___% correct	___% correct	___% correct	___% correct	___% correct	___% correct	___% correct
Elementary Spelling Inventory: number correct/Level (3 times/year)										

Individual Student Monthly Progress Monitoring Chart for *Caught Reading* (Full Calendar Year)

Student's Name _____

	AUG.	SEPT.	OCT.	NOV.	DEC.	JAN.	FEB.	MAR.	APRIL	MAY	JUNE	JULY
	Student assessment within Levels. Record information for all Levels in which a student works during the year.											
Caught Reading Level	% correct	% correct	% correct	% correct	% correct	% correct	% correct	% correct	% correct	% correct	% correct	% correct
After Midway Novel: Comprehension Check (TM)	% correct	% correct	% correct	% correct	% correct	% correct	% correct	% correct	% correct	% correct	% correct	% correct
After Midway Novel: Midway Assessment (page ___)	% correct	% correct	% correct	% correct	% correct	% correct	% correct	% correct	% correct	% correct	% correct	% correct
Average scores during month for Practice Lessons	% correct	% correct	% correct	% correct	% correct	% correct	% correct	% correct	% correct	% correct	% correct	% correct
After Final Novel: Comprehension Check (TM)	% correct	% correct	% correct	% correct	% correct	% correct	% correct	% correct	% correct	% correct	% correct	% correct
After Final Novel: Final Assessment (page ___)	% correct	% correct	% correct	% correct	% correct	% correct	% correct	% correct	% correct	% correct	% correct	% correct
	Student assessment beyond Worktext/Levels											
Highest Fluency Check for month/ WPM+comp. score	WPM = ___ Score ___ correct	WPM = ___ Score ___ correct	WPM = ___ Score ___ correct	WPM = ___ Score ___ correct	WPM = ___ Score ___ correct	WPM = ___ Score ___ correct	WPM = ___ Score ___ correct	WPM = ___ Score ___ correct	WPM = ___ Score ___ correct	WPM = ___ Score ___ correct	WPM = ___ Score ___ correct	WPM = ___ Score ___ correct
High Frequency Words: % correct	% correct	% correct	% correct	% correct	% correct	% correct	% correct	% correct	% correct	% correct	% correct	% correct
Elementary Spelling Inventory: number correct/Level (3 times/year)												

Stop and Look! What does student know/is student able to do? (rows 2–6, Jan. area)

Final Summary—Next Steps (July column)

Monthly Class Summary Chart

CIRCLE ONE: August September October November December January February March April May June July

If Levels change during a month, write new Level next to accompanying scores.

Name	Level	Midway Novel Comprehension Check*	Midway Novel Assessment Check*	Average Scores for Practice Lessons	Final Novel Comprehension Check*	Final Novel Assessment Check	Fluency Check: Highest Official WPM/Page #	High Frequency Words: Number of Words Mastered

*These columns may not need to be filled in every month, depending on rate of progress through a Level.

Fluency Check Student Recording Chart (Levels 1–3)

Directions: (1) Figure your words per minute rate—WPM (number of words divided by time); (2) Correct your answers for the Comprehension Check and make your score a percentage; and (3) Put your percentage in the box on the same row as your WPM and in the same column as the passage you read. If you did not finish reading when your teacher told you to stop, record your score on the comprehension questions in the bottom row.

Name _____ Period _____ Starting Date _____

Date									
Level	1	1	1	1	2	2	2	3	3	3
Page #	22	24	40	59–60	24	45	55–56	24	40–41	48–49
Total Word Count	162	156	215	294	195	291	417	314	439	435
200										
195										
190										
185										
180										
175										
170										
165										
160										
155										
150										
145										
140										
135										
130										
125										
120										
115										
110										
105										
100										
95										
90										
85										
80										
75										
70										
65										
60										
Below 60										

© Pearson Education, Inc. or its affiliate(s). All rights reserved.

Fluency Check Student Recording Chart (Levels 4–7)

DIRECTIONS: (1) Figure your words per minute rate—WPM (number of words divided by time); (2) Correct your answers for the Comprehension Check and make your score a percentage; (3) Put your percentage in the box on the same row as your WPM and in the same column as the passage you read. If you did not finish reading when your teacher told you to stop, record your score on the comprehension questions in the bottom row.

Name _____ Period _____ Starting Date _____

Date												
Level	4	4	4	5	5	5	6	6	6	7	7	7	7
Page #	20	43	64–65	13–14	25–26	51–52	22–23	32–33	54–55	21–23	40–41	51–52	60–62
Total Word Count	369	305	438	349	228	566	419	498	980	709	793	712	824
200													
195													
190													
185													
180													
175													
170													
165													
160													
155													
150													
145													
140													
135													
130													
125													
120													
115													
110													
105													
100													
95													
90													
85													
80													
75													
70													
65													
60													
Below 60													

High Frequency Words Mastery Chart

There are seven word list quizzes in each Level. Record your percent correct for each quiz.

Student _____

Test Name	Caught Reading Level						
	1	2	3	4	5	6	7
QUIZ 1	____%	____%	____%	____%	____%	____%	____%
QUIZ 2	____%	____%	____%	____%	____%	____%	____%
QUIZ 3	____%	____%	____%	____%	____%	____%	____%
QUIZ 4	____%	____%	____%	____%	____%	____%	____%
QUIZ 5	____%	____%	____%	____%	____%	____%	____%
QUIZ 6	____%	____%	____%	____%	____%	____%	____%
QUIZ 7	____%	____%	____%	____%	____%	____%	____%

Use this space to record words you need to study for 100 percent mastery of each Level. Cross them off when you can spell them quickly and automatically on the word list quiz.

LEVEL 1	LEVEL 2	LEVEL 3	LEVEL 4	LEVEL 5	LEVEL 6	LEVEL 7

BIBLIOGRAPHY

- Adams, M.J. (1990). Beginning to Read: Thinking and Learning About Print. Cambridge, MA: MIT Press.
- Allen, J. (2000). *Yellow Brick Roads: Shared and Guided Paths to Independent Reading 4–12.* Portland, ME: Stenhouse.
- Baker, S., Simmons, D., and Kameenui, E. (1998). *Vocabulary Acquisition: Curricular and Instructional Implications for Diverse Learners.* National Center to Improve the Tools for Educators. University of Oregon.
- Bear, D.R., Invernizzi, M., Templeton, S., and Johnston, F. (2003). *Words Their Way: Word Study for Phonics, Vocabulary, and Spelling Instruction,* 3rd ed. Upper Saddle River, NJ: Prentice Hall.
- Cohen, K. (1999). Reluctant 8th Grade Readers Enjoy Sustained Silent Reading. *California Reader,* 33(1), 22–24.
- Cunningham, P. (1999). *Phonics They Use: Words for Reading and Writing,* 3rd ed. Boston, MA: Allyn & Bacon.
- Cunningham, P. and Allington, R. (2006). *Classrooms That Work: They Can All Read and Write,* 4th ed. Boston, MA: Allyn & Bacon.
- Cuomo, G. (1962). How Fast Should a Person Read? *Saturday Review Magazine,* 3, 62–64.
- Daneman, M. (1991). Individual Differences in Reading Skills. In R. Barr, M.L. Kam: I.P. Mosenthal, and P.D. Pearson (eds.), *Handbook of Reading Research* (Vol. II, pp 512–538). White Plains, NY: Longman.
- Dowhower, S. L. (1987). Effects of Repeated Reading on Second Grade Transitional Readers' Fluency and Comprehension. *Reading Research Quarterly.* 22 (4), 389–405.
- Hoyt, L. (1998). *Revisit, Reflect, Retell: Strategies for Improving Reading Comprehension.* Portsmouth, NH: Heinemann.
- Johns, J. (2005). *Basic Reading Inventory: Pre-Primer Through Grade Twelve and Early Literacy Assessments,* 9th ed. Dubuque, Iowa: Kendall/Hunt Publishing Company.
- Mooney, M. (1990). *Reading To, With, and by Children.* Katonah, NY: Richard C. Owen Publishing.
- Moore, D., Bean T., Birdshaw, D., and Rycik, J. (1999). Adolescent Literacy: A Position Statement. *IRA Journal of Adolescent and Adult Literacy,* 43(1), 97–112.
- Pilgreen, J. (2000). *The SSR Handbook: How to Organize and Manage a Sustained Silent Reading Program.* Portsmouth, NH: Boynton/Cook.
- Robb, L. (2000). *Teaching Reading in Middle School: Grades 5 and Up.* New York, NY: Scholastic.
- Samuels, S.J. (1997). The Method of Repeated Readings. *The Reading Teacher.* 50, 376–381.
- Samuels, S.J., Schermer, N., and Reinking, D. (1992). Reading Fluency. Techniques for Making Decoding Automatic. *What Research Has to Say About Reading Instruction.* Newark, DE: International Reading Association.
- Sanacore, J. (1996). An Important Literacy Event Through the Grades. *Journal of Adolescent and Adult Literacy,* 39, 588–591.
- Schoenbach, R., Greenleaf, C., Cziko, C., and Hurwitz, L. (1999). *Reading for Understanding.* San Francisco, CA: Jossey-Bass.
- Stanovich, K. (1986). Matthew Effects in Reading: Some Consequences of Individual Differences in the Acquisition of Literacy. *Reading Research Quarterly,* 21(4), 360–406.
- Tompkins, G.E. (2005). *Literacy for the 21st Century: A Balanced Approach.* 4th ed. Upper Saddle River, NJ: Merrill/Prentice Hall.
- Trelease, J. (2001). *The Read-Aloud Handbook.* 5th ed. New York, NY: Penguin USA.
- Wood, K. (1998). Helping Struggling Readers Read. *Middle School Journal,* 29, (5).
- Wood, K. (1992). Paired Retellings from the Value of Verbal Rehearsal. (handout).